*GLOSSOLALIA*

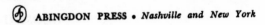

ABINGDON PRESS • *Nashville and New York*

# GLOSSOLALIA Tongue Speaking in
## Biblical, Historical, and Psychological Perspective

Frank Stagg
E. Glenn Hinson
Wayne E. Oates

**GLOSSOLALIA**

*Copyright © 1967 by Abingdon Press*

*Library of Congress Catalog Card Number: 67-22167*

SET UP, PRINTED, AND BOUND BY THE
PARTHENON PRESS, AT NASHVILLE,
TENNESSEE, UNITED STATES OF AMERICA

**To**
The Faculty of the
Southern Baptist Theological Seminary
with our gratitude for their dialogue
in the understood Word of God

# CONTENTS

# CONTENTS

# Why a Book on Glossolalia Today?

*E. Glenn Hinson*

Is the "speaking-in-tongues" movement in the churches today something that should be taken seriously? Much has been said about it, but more needs to be said. Glossolalia is a subjective experience. However, an objective but understanding treatment of the subject in a nonpartisan way is needed. That is the concern of this book.

Certainly a lot has been written and said, both by persons involved in the charismatic revival and by those outside. From insiders there are, for example, four widely circulated periodicals—*Trinity, Voice, View,* and *Vision*—which address themselves exclusively to the issue; pamphlets which describe what has happened among Baptists, Episcopalians, Methodists, and Presbyterians; histories, autobiographies or biographies like John Sherrill's *They Speak with Other Tongues;* and numerous private publications. From outsiders there are innumerable articles about one or another aspect of the experience, denominational studies, and a few books, in addition to studies of the older Pentecostalism.

As extensive as these may seem, however, the extent and continued success of the new Pentecostalism make it a still live issue. To borrow an analogy from Yale student David Fischer, writing home to his parents about his experience with tongues, it is "like driving a nitroglycerine truck down a dirt road." [1] Without carefully informed opinions, the development may become increasingly disruptive and divisive, for already several denominations and individuals have suffered severely because of rash action on the part of leaders and equally rash reactions on the part of those who foster the charismatic approach.

Involved in this confusion, however, is a certain one-sidedness in evaluating a complex problem. The intricacy of the whole affair requires that it be considered from no less than three sides—biblical-theological, historical, and psychological—a formidable task for one person. To my knowledge, only Morton Kelsey and denominational studies have attempted this. Accordingly, it seemed wise to two of my colleagues and me to coordinate our efforts, first in a symposium at Faculty Club of the Southern Baptist Theological Seminary and then in the following essays. Dr. Frank Stagg has evaluated the biblical evidence, I the historical, and Dr. Wayne E. Oates the psychological. Our aim is to interpret the phenomenon of tongue speaking from these three sides. In that we offer an interpretation from a trifold perspective, we hope, whether by chance or by design, to cast here and there a new beam of light on some obscure aspects of the charisma of glossolalia, whether new or old.

## THE STORY OF THE MOVEMENT

Glossolalia or tongue speaking, once confined almost exclusively to the Pentecostal churches, has, within about a decade or so, become quite widespread among non-Pentecostals. The first general public notice of it was taken in 1960, when the Reverend Dennis Bennett, Rector of a thriving Episcopal church in Van Nuys, California, resigned rather than see his congregation fractured by a debate over its practice by him and members of the congregation. But this report merely signaled the *public* debut of a movement which had been going on in private for some time. For, overnight, reports of similar experiences cropped up almost everywhere, dating back to the fifties, previously suppressed perhaps for fear of denominational censure and because of uncertainty about the experience.

It is difficult to say where, when, and how the new movement was born. Those who report glossolalia today usually ascribe the experience to prayer and laying-on-of-hands by one who had previously had "the baptism of the Spirit"; consequently, I suspect there must be a link with the older Pentecostalism. As a matter of fact,

11

the modern "charismatic revival," as its leaders prefer to describe it, has received no small boost from the Full Gospel Business Men's Fellowship International (FGBMFI), founded in California in 1953 by Pentecostals. Today, of course, its constituency includes men of all denominations.

It comes as no surprise, then, to hear that the first public report occurred in California and that the Reverend Mr. Bennett first came in contact with it through two lay members of a neighboring Episcopal church. Moreover, a reading of reports by other notable figures in the movement reveals that a large number either experienced tongues or heard about them through a Pentecostal friend. Not untypical is the story of Harold Bredesen, Dutch Reformed minister and now editor of *Trinity* magazine, who traces his experience to "a Pentecostal camp meeting, with sawdust floor, and all the works." [2] So even if the movement started somewhat spontaneously, which is doubtful, Pentecostals certainly deserve credit for helping to fan the sparks into a vigorous flame.

Whatever its genesis, the rapid spread of the movement is little short of miraculous. With the help of the FGBMFI, the Blessed Trinity Society, and individuals who desire zealously to share the experience with others, it has touched nearly every Protestant denomination and, the FGBMFI now reports, even Roman Catholics and Orthodox. Already by 1964 some California members claimed that eleven percent of all Episcopalians, Presbyterians, and Baptists had experienced "the baptism of the Spirit." Although this figure is undoubtedly a gross exaggeration, there can be no doubt, judging solely from the obvious concern of many denominational leaders, that a large number of their constituency have been swept up into the Pentecostal tide.

In spite of warnings by denominational leaders and the removal of pastors from their charges, the movement rolls on. The periodicals published by the FGBMFI continue to carry regular reports of pastors and laymen who have received the gift of tongues. Indeed, the movement seems to gain increasing confidence as time passes.

Increasing confidence is due, in part, to the fact that the movement has made inroads into certain intellectual centers of America. It is a matter of some pride to the neo-Pentecostals, and widely publicized by them, that Yale experienced a Pentecostal revival in October, 1961, when about twenty students and one faculty member received "the baptism of the Spirit" and spoke in tongues. From Yale the movement spread to Dartmouth, Princeton, and other university campuses across the nation.

The enlisting of intellectuals has proved a great boon for the movement in several ways. In 1963, the FGBMFI initiated a series of seminars, conducted by a cross section of its leaders in the various denominations, like Dennis Bennett; Harold Bredesen; Howard Ervin, Pastor of Emmanuel Baptist Church in Atlantic City, New Jersey; and Robert Rice, Presbyterian missionary to Korea and Princeton doctoral student. The first seminar drew 170 students from more than thirty colleges and seminaries. Perhaps of greater significance than the seminars, however, the enlisting of intellectuals provided high caliber

13

apologists. In 1959 the FGBMFI launched a new publication, called *View,* with a much more intellectual thrust than its earlier periodicals, *Voice* and *Vision.* Whereas the latter sought to channel reports of experiences, the former discusses the theology, history, and relevance of charismatic gifts in modern society.

As it has assumed greater intellectual respectability, the charismatic revival has also gained the financial means to sustain its varied projects. Not a few of those who have recorded their experiences are people of substantial wealth. The president of FGBMFI, Demos Shakarian, for example, is a wealthy dairyman-grocer, whose personal story sounds like that of Horatio Alger. This is a far cry from impoverished Pentecostalism of old.

Furthermore, the movement has attracted socially prominent people who have helped greatly to enhance its reputation. One of these is M. G. "Pat" Robertson, son of former Virginia Senator A. Willis Robertson. The young Robertson, who for some time had been seeking such a religious experience, attending numerous meetings and consulting with leaders in the movement, broke out in "tongues" after his child was delivered from a high fever after prayer. As a result of his religious experiences, Robertson has established a "Christian Television Station" at Portsmouth, Virginia, and hopes to develop a "Christian Broadcasting Network."

## WHY ITS SUCCESS?

The unusual success of the charismatic revival prompts one to inquire further into the nature of the experiences recorded. In making such an investigation, it would certainly be hazardous to generalize, typing all experiences in one or more categories. Nevertheless, some elements in the reports seem to appear so consistently, almost without exception, that a general statement can be attempted.

In almost all cases, the recipients of the gift of tongues have spoken of a "feeling" of power which preceded the experience. Frequently, they compare this feeling to electricity. As they have sought to interpret the experience, they have related it invariably to the charismatic gifts mentioned along with tongues by Paul in I Corinthians. However, some distinction is usually made between the *initial* experience and subsequent use of the gift of tongues. For example, in answer to a student's question in the first seminar, held in New York City in 1963, it was admitted that not all had this as a *gift,* that is, for continuous use; rather, some would have only the *initial* experience.[3]

With respect to the nature of the language itself, there are claims both to speak "unknown" tongues, glossolalia in the strict sense, and "other" tongues, foreign languages. However much weight Pentecostals or neo-Pentecostals place on the latter, though, they seldom give evidence of more than an occasional word or brief phrases. When examined by expert linguists, longer speeches, recorded on tape, have turned out to be mixtures of glossolalia with no more than a genuine foreign word thrown in here or there, giving clear proof that the person had not really received the ability to speak another language.

That which probably helps to explain the movement's success most readily, however, has to do neither with feeling nor language, but with something genuinely religious. Among other things, "the baptism of the Spirit" has reportedly resulted in improved morality, in the cessation of alcoholism, in the integration of disturbed personalities, in the curing of various psychological or even physiological disorders, in the restoration of marital harmony, and in the revitalizing of Christian fellowship within the churches. In brief, people and churches have "found" themselves through the experience. So, even if these consequences were not typical of the whole movement, they would certainly appeal to men and women of churches everywhere who seek solutions to problems like these.

## WHAT DOES IT ALL MEAN?

This raises at once the question of meaning. Were tongue speakers able to cite only their private "feelings" or "speakings," they would probably go largely unnoticed. But because more dramatic things are happening, they have gained a hearing. What is to be said about the movement?

Like most debatable matters, this one has at least two sides. On the one side, those who have had the experience of tongues interpret it as part of a great charismatic revival which, they hope, will sweep across America and even the world, bringing to an end the advance of secularism and restoring to a weak and seriously fragmented church its vitality and unity. Dennis Bennett, certainly one of the more articulate exponents, has stated the case in this way: The church is in a mess, organized Christianity "a failure." Why? Because the Holy Spirit has not had a fair chance to work experientially in the church. What should be done? Sit down and ask people who have had an experience of the Holy Spirit what to do. It is time to stop relying on intellectual analyses and to start relying on spiritual experiences. After all, Christianity is "not an intellectual matter at all. It is a purely personal and spiritual matter." [4] As far as the church is concerned, then, it must again become the church depicted in the Book of Acts, namely, letting the Holy Spirit hold sway. Speaking in tongues, therefore, is not the central issue, though it is real. It is a manifestation of what really happens when the Spirit takes hold.

On the other side, there is a mixture of anxiety, bewilderment, and hostility. Denominational leaders have not known quite how to interpret what they see and hear, nor what to do in response. If the occurrence were purely a novelty, with neither scriptural nor historical evidence for it, it could be readily shunted aside and those who reported it restrained. Unfortunately, as is often true in Christian life, such is not the case. In fact, the Scriptures give considerable attention to the matter, the apostle Paul going so far as to confess that he himself had experienced "tongues" (I Cor. 14:18). In Acts, Luke implies that tongue speaking occurred regularly in the primitive church, and the phenomenon has turned up spasmodically in its later history.

The problem is made more sticky by the fact that religious experience, by its very nature, is somewhat intangible. What responsible Christian leader does not fear that he may "quench the Spirit," if he makes dogmatic judgments about prophecies and revelations? He cannot help but remember the persecution of the prophets and saints by leaders who failed to understand them or God's message. What's more, Protestantism itself, in all of its diversity, emerged from spiritual convictions which others did not acknowledge but which form the very warp and woof of Protestant faith.

With so many complex factors involved in the subject, it is not surprising that reports on it have been somewhat indecisive and have reflected divergent attitudes. After study by a Commission of the Division of Pastoral Services of the Department of Ministry, Bishop James A. Pike, in whose diocese glossolalia was first reported, issued a stern warning concerning the practice of it and forbade its encouragement by the clergy, contending that it represented "heresy in embryo." While admitting that the movement indicated "a real need and hunger for a more vital, Spirit-filled Christian experience in life," he directed his constituency to seek the normal channels of Word and Sacrament in order to enhance their religious experience.[5]

A report published after a two-year study in December, 1963, by an eight-member committee of the American Lutheran Church reflected a somewhat different attitude. It acknowledged the scriptural basis of tongue speaking "as one of several gifts of the Holy Spirit" and refused to forbid its private exercise "for the individual's personal edification."

The most thorough study produced to date, Episcopal Rector Morton Kelsey's *Tongue Speaking*, has cast the phenomenon in a rather favorable light. Although conceding certain negative aspects—divisiveness, disorderliness, and so on—and confessing even that it is "dangerous," he still insists that the case is not closed. Glossolalia has made demonstrable positive contributions, as indicated above. In the final analysis, Kelsey concludes after extensive biblical, historical, and psychological research, as one of the gifts of the Spirit, it can make a contribution to the individual and to the Christian community, if exercised discreetly and with humility within the community. "It is," he notes in conclusion, "one entrance into the spiritual realm; by giving access to the unconscious, it is one contact with non-physical reality which allows God to speak directly to man." [6]

What is submitted in this book grew out of a program of the Faculty Club of the Southern Baptist Theological Seminary in which the three writers were asked to provide a panel discussion on the subject of glossolalia. Spurred by discussions within the Faculty Club and by the continuing movement in the Christian world, the three of us agreed to develop our papers into fuller essays, following out our original assignments in terms of biblical, historical, and psychological analyses.

# Glossolalia in the New Testament

*Frank Stagg*

"Speaking in tongues" is the popular phrase for what scholars term glossolalia. This phenomenon, appearing from time to time in the Christian world, is unmistakably reflected in the New Testament. To some it is a sign of church renewal and is to be cultivated. To others it offers only dubious rewards to some individuals, cell groups, and sectarians but leaves disillusionment and disunity in its wake. To some it is the gift of the Holy Spirit, offering a new dimension in Christian fulfillment. To others it is an egocentric escape from the heavier demands of the Christian calling and is more damaging than helpful to the body of Christ and to its witness and work in the world. Some point to the "good" it does; others point to the "harm" it does.

Although the fact of glossolalia in the early church is clearly reflected in the New Testament, the more difficult questions are those about its antecedents, origin, nature, extent, and significance. Of primary importance is the question of the relationship between what occurred at Jerusalem on the day of Pentecost (Acts 2) and the practice at Corinth (I Cor. 12–14).

Except for Acts and I Corinthians, there are no explicit references to "speaking in tongues" in the New Testament, Mark 16:17 being generally recognized as a late addition to the Gospel of Mark. Acts refers to "other tongues" (2:4) and to "tongues" (10:46; 19:6), these three occurrences coinciding with crucial junctures in Christian history, i.e., the breakthrough of the gospel to Jews, God-fearing Gentiles, and some followers of John the Baptist who until then had not followed Christ. First Corinthians mentions "kinds of tongues" (12:10, 28), "interpretation of tongues" (12:10), "strange tongues" (14:21), and "tongue" or "tongues" (12:30; 13:1, 8; 14:2, 4, 5, 6, 9, 13, 14, 18, 19, 22, 23, 26, 27, 39). There is no Greek word for "unknown" in I Cor. 14:2, 4, 13, 14, 19, 27. The King James Version puts "unknown" in italics, its way of acknowledging that there is no word for it in the Greek text.

## "GLOSSA" IN NEW TESTAMENT USAGE

The noun "glossolalia" does not appear in the New Testament; but the phrase "to speak with tongues" (*glōssais lalein*) appears, and there are frequent occurrences of the word *glossa*, a component of the term glossolalia. Although *glossa* is commonly translated "tongue," hence *glossa* (tongue) and *lalia* (speaking) for "speaking in tongues," actually the term is employed in at least three different ways: (1) for the physiological organ of taste or speech, (2) for language itself or a manner of speech, and (3) for strange or obscure speech.[1]

*Glossa* unmistakably refers to the tongue as an organ of speech in Luke 16:24, where the rich man in torment wants water for his tongue. It is used in the literal sense here and elsewhere (cf. Mark 7:33, 35; Luke 1:64; Rom. 3:13; 14:11; I Cor. 14:9; Jas. 3:5-6; I John 3:18; I Peter 3:10; and Rev. 16:10). In Acts 2:3 it is used in a figurative sense for forked flames of fire.[2] *Glossa* is used in a figurative sense or personified sense in Acts 2:26, "my tongue rejoiced," and in Phil. 2:11, "every tongue confess." [3]

A second usage for *glossa* is found in Acts and Revelation. In Acts 2:11 the plural of *glossa* is used for language, where the statement "we hear them telling in our own tongues" parallels vs. 8, "we hear, each of us in his own native language." Manuscripts in Acts 2:6 differ, some having "dialect" and some "tongues," whether or not with different meaning is not clear. The book of Revelation follows Old Testament precedent in employing *glossa* for language in a figurative or personified sense, using it as a synonym for "tribe," "people," and "nation" (5:9; 7:9; 10:11; 11:9; 13:7; 14:6; and 17:15).[4] In this usage, "tongue simply distinguishes one linguistic group of people from another.

The third usage is most difficult, where *glossa* is used for strange or obscure speech or utterance, now commonly called glossolalia. This usage is found in I Cor. 12:10, 28, 30; 13:1, 8; 14:1-27, 39; and Acts 10:46; 19:6. It will be a major concern of this essay to question whether or not this usage is to be found in a source underlying the second chapter of Acts (particularly 2:4) and obscured by Luke, as is widely held. The implications of each conclusion will be pursued, i.e., that Luke correctly represents the "tongues" at Pentecost as intelligible language, or that he deliberately or unknowingly obscured an older tradition that the "speaking in tongues" at Pentecost was unintelligible, ecstatic utterance.

## THE TEXTUAL CASE FOR MARK 16:17

Before turning to the essay's major concern with I Cor. 12–14 and the book of Acts, it is necessary to examine Mark 16:17, the only other New Testament reference requiring serious consideration with respect to "speaking with tongues." Mark 16:17, "they will speak in new tongues," is used as a basic text by some tongues movements; but it is not original to Mark. Although it reflects a later period's interest in glossolalia, it does not properly belong to the study of glossolalia in the New Testament.

Textual critics are almost unanimous in the judgment that the authentic text of Mark ends at 16:8.[5] Either this was the original ending to the Gospel of Mark, or the original ending has been lost. The most reliable

23

manuscripts in Greek, Latin, and Syriac are supported by the Armenian, Ethiopian, and Georgian versions and early church fathers, like Clement of Alexandria (ca. 200), Origen (ca. 230), Eusebius (ca. 340), and Jerome (d. 420), in concluding Mark at 16:8. The now traditional ending with 16:9-20 was known as early as the latter half of the second century (Justin possibly, Tatian, Irenaeus, Hippolytus, Celsus possibly, Hesychius), and it was widely accepted by the end of the fourth century; but external and internal evidence indicate that it was added to Mark to complete what seemed to be an abrupt ending. Two other short endings and several combinations of spurious endings are found, weakening the case for anything authentic beyond 16:8.

The "long ending" (16:9-20), although not original to Mark, is significant in its reflection of second-century theological interests. Brought together in emphasis are baptismal regeneration, exorcism of demons, speaking in tongues, snake handling, drinking poison, and healing of the sick:

He who believes and is baptized will be saved; but he who does not believe will be condemned. And these signs will accompany those who believe: in my name they will cast out demons; they will speak in new tongues; they will pick up serpents, and if they drink any deadly thing, it will not hurt them; they will lay their hands on the sick; and they will recover.

For the study of the New Testament, however, this passage is not directly relevant.

24

## THE PROBLEMS OF ACTS 2

Taken at face value, Luke's account of the gift of tongues in Jerusalem on the day of Pentecost seems clear enough (Acts 2). Almost all interpreters understand that Luke represents the tongues on the day of Pentecost to have been understandable language of some kind. What was spoken was intelligible to "devout men from every nation under heaven" (2:5). Those dwelling at Jerusalem were astounded that, as Galilean disciples spoke, each heard the language (dialect) of his birth (2:7-8). The disagreement arises over the question of Luke's trustworthiness in the narrative.

Many scholars[6] contend that Luke's account is secondary, not conforming to what actually occurred at Jerusalem. They argue that shining through Luke's narrative are reflections of an older story which held that the phenomenon at Pentecost was ecstatic and unintelligible, like that which Paul later encountered at Corinth. They see Luke either consciously seeking to obscure the fact that the earliest glossolalia in Jerusalem was ecstatic utterance, representing it as being understandable language, or unknowingly employing a secondary source which already had altered the picture of glossolalia at Jerusalem. One theory holds that Luke's theological bias overrode the tradition with which he worked. The other view holds that Luke was misinformed by his sources. What are the evidences, and to what conclusion do they point? These questions must be met, not evaded.

Yet another theory is that Acts has gone through at least two recensions, a Proto-Acts having been enlarged to our present Acts. Proponents of this view differ in their reconstruction of the alleged Proto-Acts and in what they see to have been added by the redactor, but all make room for the theory that Proto-Acts knew nothing of a miracle of speech or hearing which resulted in the understandable language of our present Acts 2.

We must focus upon these questions: (1) Was the phenomenon at Pentecost like or unlike the ecstatic, unintelligible utterance at Corinth? (2) Was the Corinthian expression a deviation from the Pentecostal gift, or is Luke's account of the Pentecostal experience a secondary version which hides what really occurred? How we answer these questions affects our understanding and assessment of "tongues" today.

## THE STORY IN ACTS 2

As the story reaches us in Acts 2, the gift of tongues was a miracle of speech or hearing by which Jewish pilgrims of various linguistic backgrounds were able to understand, each in his native language, what was said by those upon whom the Holy Spirit came. The fact of understanding is what Luke emphasizes. He does not explain how this was possible. One might speculate that various languages were spoken, at least Aramaic and Greek, or that only dialectical variations of one language were involved. But this does not satisfy the implications of the story as Luke tells it. Luke seems to imply that there was an understanding made possible not by the linguistic competence of the hearers but by the power of the Holy Spirit. The amazement which

Luke attributes to the worshipers at Jerusalem is not traceable to their finding multiple languages at Jerusalem, for there was nothing unusual about that, as public inscriptions in Hebrew, Greek, and Latin attest.[7]

Whatever one's judgment of Luke's accuracy may be, he cannot validly overlook Luke's obvious intention to represent a miraculous occurrence at Pentecost. The language employed implies a phenomenon not understandable on natural grounds. There was the gift of the Holy Spirit; there were audio and visual signs like wind from heaven and tongues of fire; and it was the Spirit who "gave them utterance" as they "began to speak in other tongues" (2:1-4).

Scholars who hold that the phenomenon described by Luke was actually unintelligible, ecstatic utterance, changed by Luke or some secondary source which he employed into intelligible speech, point to the charge made by some scoffers that the speakers were "filled with new wine" (2:13). They observe that at Pentecost and at Corinth some understood and some did not, assuming that the "interpretation of tongues" (I Cor. 12:10, 30; 14:26-27) means the same thing as hearing in one's own language (Acts 2:6, 11). They also observe the comparison of the gift of the Spirit at Pentecost and Caesarea (10:45 ff.; 11:15-16). These are far-reaching conclusions, built upon evidence too strong to be ignored yet far from conclusive. Other evidences in the narrative support Luke's position.

According to 2:15 ff., Peter not only denied the charge of drunkenness but also identified this speaking with prophecy. He saw the coming of the Holy Spirit as fulfillment of the promise found in the prophet Joel [8] when he spoke of the outpouring of the Spirit in the last days, accompanied by prophesying (inspired preaching), the seeing of visions and dreaming of dreams, and signs from heaven. Peter related this to the speaking of those charged with drunkenness, not simply to the sermon he was about to preach (2:17-21). Furthermore, Peter related this to evangelism, prophetic preaching designed to lead men to call upon the Lord that they might be saved (2:17, 18, 21). This does not imply "ecstatic egoism" or justify the conclusion that the historical kernel of Luke's story is "a mass ecstasy on the part of the disciples which includes outbreaks of glossolalia." [9]

Paul clearly distinguished between tongues and prophecy, the former unintelligible and the latter intelligible (I Cor. 12:10-11, 29-30; 13:1-2; 14:1-6, 22). Acts 2 identifies the phenomenon at Pentecost with prophecy, not with unintelligible, ecstatic utterance. To seize upon the drunkenness charge as an authentic echo of the true story and to charge Luke with confusion is highly precarious. However, should one choose that road, he will have to travel it to its end. He will have to risk giving up more than Luke's version of "intelligible language"; he may have to give up Peter's sermon, the conversion of three thousand persons, and much else which is included in Acts 2, for current source theories find all of Acts 2 built upon a secondary, legendary source. If the drunkenness charge overturns Luke's position that the tongues were understandable, it also calls in question his position that Peter joined the gift of the Spirit and

"Pentecost" as a whole with prophecy and evangelism, for Luke's version of tongues and his story of Peter's prophetic preaching go together. On the two-source theory, the whole story of "Pentecost" comes under question. It is to the problem of sources that we must now give closer attention, for much is at stake.

## SOURCES AND ACTS 2

In a recent source-critical study of Luke and Acts, A. Q. Morton and G. H. C. MacGregor claim that there was a Proto-Acts and that it began with 1:12-14; 3:1-10; and 4:1–5:12a.[10] According to this thesis, Acts did not originally contain 1:1-11; 1:15–2:47; 3:11-26; or 5:12b-42, these passages being assigned to an inferior source. Upon this reconstruction, Acts 4:31 is seen to be the earliest description of what occurred in Jerusalem: "And when they had prayed, the place in which they were gathered together was shaken; and they were all filled with the Holy Spirit and spoke the word of God with boldness." This text, acknowledged by all as primary, connects normal speech with the gift of the Holy Spirit!

By the reconstruction of Morton and MacGregor, the whole second chapter of Acts is eliminated as a primary source. The theory leaves no explicit support in Acts for unintelligible speech at Pentecost, for it eliminates Pentecost itself, unless it is implied in 4:31 where speech is normal. The chief reliance of Morton and MacGregor is upon the electronic computer, with special attention given to length of paragraphs as a criterion for distinguishing sources and the hand of the redactor in Luke and Acts.

The electronic computer method of isolating sources and identifying authorship is new and unproven. Although serviceable within limits, it cannot stand alone in the ambitious task in which Morton and MacGregor have employed it. If, despite the limits of the method, they are correct in their analysis, then Acts 2 is irrelevant to the study of glossolalia except as it reflects a later redactional interest. I am unconvinced by Morton and MacGregor and by older source theories relating to Acts 2; but the argument here is that Acts 2 cannot be used in two ways, both to reject Luke's account as untrustworthy and at the same time build upon a part of what is judged to be a secondary source.

Source analysis in Acts is not new. For nearly two centuries Acts has been subjected to source analysis by scores of scholars working in the German, French, and English languages.[11] The search for sources is a valid one, but nothing like consensus has been achieved. In my judgment, until something more conclusive is demonstrated, the Lucan account in Acts as we have it must be our working base.

*Conclusions from Source Analysis.* A few conclusions may be drawn from this consideration of source theories for Acts: (1) One may not use Acts both ways, rejecting its story of "tongues" as intelligible utterance yet accepting uncritically its account of the outpouring of the Holy Spirit on a certain day of Pentecost, the great missionary sermon of Peter on the same day, the accompaniment of miracles, the winning of three thousand converts, teaching, and the beautiful *koinonia* of the disciples, for these too belong to the "source" in question. (2) If the original story (source A) held that the manifestation in Jerusalem was ecstatic glossolalia (as at Corinth), then Luke represents a church tradition which found this sufficiently problematic to reject it in favor of intelligible polyglossia. (3) If, as held by source critics from Harnack to Morton and MacGregor, Acts 4:31 is our earliest description of the giving of the Holy Spirit, then the giving of the Holy Spirit was bound up with power manifested in the normal speaking of the Word of God, with no reference to Pentecost or glossolalia in any form. (4) The story in its present form clearly represents the Pentecostal gift as intelligible speech (polyglossia), with only possible echoes of another tradition. (5) Under no defensible reconstruction may one validly dignify the Corinthian type of ecstatic utterance with the Pentecostal factors of prophecy, evangelism, teaching, and *koinonia*.

## SIGNIFICANCE OF TONGUES IN ACTS 2

Luke represented the gift of tongues at Pentecost as something unique, a miracle of communication. Whether the miracle was that of speech or hearing or both is not clear. The equivalence of speaking "in other tongues" (2:4) with "each of us in his own native language" (2:8) indicates that intelligible speech was meant. Luke's primary interest is not in tongues but in the empowering of the church by the Holy Spirit. Just as in the Gospel of Luke (1:15, 35, 41, 67; 2:26; 3:22) the birth of Jesus

31

is told in the context of the Holy Spirit's activity, so in Acts the birth or empowering of the church is set forth in relationship with the Holy Spirit.[12]

Did Luke represent the Pentecostal gift of tongues as corresponding to the giving of the Law at Mount Sinai? A rabbinical tradition says that when God gave the Law at Sinai, his voice was heard in all the languages (seventy) of the world, and another Jewish tradition holds that the Law was given on the day of Pentecost (cf. *Tanhuma* 26*c* and *Pesahim* 68*b*). The suggestion comes readily that Luke saw a parallel to this in the gift of tongues, the gospel being preached to the whole world on this particular day of Pentecost.

Several problems confront this theory. In the first place, there is no certain evidence that these rabbinical traditions were known in Luke's time. They may not be earlier than the second century of the Christian era. Then, too, there are at least two significant differences between the rabbinical traditions and Luke's narrative. Luke's story has to do with the preaching of the gospel, making no reference to the Law.[13] Again, Luke represents those who heard the disciples' "speaking with tongues" and Peter's sermon as being Jews (2:5, 10, 14, 22, 36), not Gentiles.

Paralleling gospel with law would not be a difficult adaptation for Luke, and two things may be said about the reference to Jews instead of all nations. In the first place, "Jews" is omitted in Codex Sinaiticus (fourth century) and appears in a different word order in Codex Ephraemi (fifth century). Lake [14] suggests that "Jews" is not original and that the multitude at Pentecost represented the whole world, Jewish and heathen alike, the writer of Acts seeing the preaching at Pentecost as the beginning of the world mission contemplated in 1:8. Haenchen suggests that Luke may have seen the tongues of fire as each representing or conferring a language and that this may have been his adaptation of yet another Jewish tradition which related tongues of fire and the giving of the Law to a grain festival.[15]

Haenchen sees Luke's emphasis upon the Holy Spirit as a parallel to God's initial work in creation. Just as God breathed his breath into man at the creation, so the new man is created by the inbreathing of the Holy Spirit.[16] Thus the new creation is brought about as was the creation of man in the beginning. Haenchen suggests that Luke's reference to Jews throughout the Pentecostal story agrees with his whole concept of the Christian mission. The Gentiles were to be reached gradually, only after the Jews had received the gospel.[17] He also sees the gift of tongues as the reversal of the confusion of tongues at Babel.[18] Just as the sinful community was fragmented at Babel and experienced such confusion of language that they could not understand one another, so at Pentecost the Spirit of Christ was uniting a fragmented humanity. The marvel of being able to understand one another contrasts with the confusion at Babel. Tongues at Pentecost stood for unity and understanding, not for confusion and disruption of fellowship as later at Corinth.

Haenchen further suggests that the Jewish hearers at Pentecost were not pilgrims who had come to Jerusalem only for the feast but that they were Diaspora Jews who had returned from all over the world to relocate in Jerusalem.[19] This would imply a uniting of mankind, beginning with these Jews. The gift of tongues would serve and reflect that purpose. Tongues at Pentecost signified the uniting of mankind, not the dividing of the church as later at Corinth.

None of these theories about background to and purpose in Acts 2 can be established. However, each theory presupposes that Luke intends that "tongues" refer to understandable language. This does not prove Luke's correctness, but it supports the view that he intended to be understood in this way.

## TONGUES ELSEWHERE IN ACTS

In only two places outside the second chapter does Acts refer to speaking in tongues, a bare mention in each case (10:46; 19:6). As in Acts 2, the emphasis is upon the coming of the Holy Spirit, not upon tongues. There may be significance in the fact that it is in the three chapters in which tongues are mentioned that the gospel breaks through to a new group: Jews, God-fearing Gentiles, and followers of John the Baptist who had not followed Christ.[20] This agrees with Luke's theme of tracing the progress of the gospel across barriers of nationality and race, struggling to be preached "unhindered" (28:31).

Whether speaking with tongues in the Caesarean home of Cornelius (10:46) and at Ephesus on the part of the followers of John the Baptist (19:6) is to be construed as ecstatic, unintelligible utterance or intelligible speech is not conclusive. There is no indication of a language barrier on either occasion, and this would seem to rule out the need for a miracle of language as Luke indicates at Pentecost.

On the other hand, those at Caesarea were heard "speaking in tongues and extolling God" (10:46), and those at Ephesus "spoke with tongues and prophesied" (19:6). Prophecy, at least, is distinguished from the ecstatic utterance at Corinth. Either two things are meant in Acts 19:6, or the speaking in tongues was intelligible, prophetic utterance as that at Jerusalem (Acts 2:15-18). That those in Caesarea were heard "speaking in tongues and extolling God" (10:46) corresponds to the tribute at Jerusalem, "we hear them telling in our own tongues the mighty works of God" (2:11). This points to intelligible speech.

## TONGUES AT CORINTH

Glossolalia is treated as a problem in I Cor. 12–14. This is significant. Although the theme of these three chapters is the gifts of the Spirit, the problems related to "tongues" dominate throughout. Paul does not encourage speaking in tongues, unless 14:5a be used in an atomistic, proof-text way. He warns against various dangers and damages related to "tongues." He set up various controls lest the practice get out of hand. He stopped short of banning glossolalia; but he rated it the least of the Spirit's gifts, and he predicted that tongues would stop (13:8).

*The Threat of Tongues.* Paul saw "tongues" as a

35

triple threat: (1) to the fellowship of the church, (2) to the persons who spoke in tongues, and (3) to the influence of the church upon the outside world. First Cor. 12 portrays the church as the body of Christ, stressing the Spirit's diversity of gifts and thus the Spirit's provision for both unity and variety in the church. Paul's laboring of the point shows that at Corinth there were spiritual pride, jealousy, and competitiveness over individual gifts. Chapter 14 indicates that much of this had to do with "tongues."

Chapter 13, the great love chapter, was composed to meet the problem of "tongues." Love is the highest "way"; and without love, speaking "with the tongues of men and of angels" is but empty sound. Love is God's excellent and ultimate way. In contrast, tongues "will cease" (13:8). Love is God's endless highway; "tongues" are a dead-end street, leading nowhere. Some gifts, like knowledge, will give way to something more mature, like child's talk giving way to man's talk, or like the reflection in a mirror giving way to face-to-face encounter; but no such promise is made for tongues. They simply stop.

Chapter 14 spells out glossolalia's limitations for good and its potential for harm. At best, one who "speaks in a tongue" speaks to God but not to men, "for no one understands him" (14:2). Tongues are contrasted with prophecy, the inspired speaking which edifies, exhorts, and comforts other people (14:3). Tongues are self-centered, concerned with one's own good; prophecy is concerned with the upbuilding of the church (14:4). Paul's main point in 14:1-19 and elsewhere is that one seek the gift of prophecy rather than that of tongues. Ecstatic, unintelligible utterance with its egoism is a poor substitute for love's concern to speak words which strengthen and unify the church.

A further damage done by "tongues" is to the church's witness to people outside the church. To them speaking in tongues is madness (14:23). Tongues are meaningless to newcomers within the church (14:16), and they repel outsiders. At best tongues are an enigma to them (14:22); at worst they persuade them that the church fosters insanity.

*Paul's Restraint.* Paul exercised restraint in what he has to say about tongues. He recognized that in some cases a genuine experience with the Spirit would be outwardly expressed in emotional, ecstatic, and unintelligible utterance. Within limits and under specified controls, "tongues" were to be respected. He did rate "tongues" as the least gift. He preferred for the church five words with understanding to ten thousand words with a tongue (14:19). The "odds" are 2000 to one!

When Paul said that he spoke in tongues more than others (14:18), he was following his familiar pattern of meeting opponents on their own ground. For example, in refuting Judaizers, he pointed out that he had a better record than they in keeping the Law (Phil. 3:1-11). If the Corinthians could boast of speaking in tongues, so could he. But he did not boast!

Paul "leaned over backwards" to be conciliatory with the Corinthians. The situation was desperate, for the church was divided, problem ridden, and many were even challenging Paul's claim to be an apostle. Many were hostile to Paul. He conceded as much as he could to those whose pride was in "tongues." But what he gave with one hand he took back with the other. Their gift was the least of all, and it was dangerous. It must be controlled. Only one was to speak at a time, not more than two or three per service, and someone must be able to interpret the meaning (14:27). Possibly the interpreter was a person who knew the speaker well enough to give the background of experience which produced the ecstatic utterance. So "tongues" were permitted, but rationed. Faith, hope, love, kindness, goodness, knowledge, self-control, evangelism, and ministry to the needy —by contrast—are not rationed.

*Unintelligible.* The "tongues" at Corinth were not languages like Aramaic, Greek, or Latin. They were motor phenomena brought on under the excitement of religious experience. They could result from a genuine encounter with God. On the other hand, "tongues" could be an effect highly desired, expected, sought, and displayed for one's own enhancement. The utterance was unintelligible. It was like the blowing of a trumpet in so garbled a way that soldiers would not know whether to arm for battle or go to bed (14:8). It was like listening to a "barbarian" whose speech conveyed no meaning (14:11). It left the understanding (*nous*) unfruitful (14:14). "Tongues" belong to the mind (*phren*) of a baby, not of a mature person (14:20). As an emotional, motor reaction, one could engage in "tongues" without use of his mind (14:19).

*A Problem-Ridden Church.* It is significant that it was at Corinth, where conduct was most disgraceful, that speaking with tongues was most prized.[21] This is not to say that "tongues" caused the disgraceful conduct or that they must appear together. It is to see that at Corinth they were compatible. There were divisions in the church (I Cor. 1:10 ff.). One man was living in incest, living illicitly with his father's wife; and the church was proud of this, presumably justifying it on the "holiness" doctrine that the "sanctified" or the "spiritual" were above sin (5:1-13; cf. Rom. 6:1-11). Church members were bringing lawsuits against one another before pagan courts, selfishly striving to see who could get what (6:1-11). Some understood grace to be license and required to be told that members of the body of Christ were not to give their bodies to harlots (6:15). There were serious marital problems in the church (chap. 7). Some were conceited over their superior "knowledge" and had to be told that love builds up while "knowledge" puffs up (chap. 8). Freedom was interpreted as personal rights and exploited to the hurt of other people (chap. 9). Some tried to be at home at the table of the Lord and the table of demons, i.e., idol feasts at pagan temples (10:14-22). Church services were disrupted and in disorder (11:1-16). Even the Lord's Supper was turned into clannish and selfish indulgences (11:17-34). The gifts of the Spirit, especially tongues, were occasions for jealousy, envy, and competitiveness (chap. 12–14). Some denied the resurrection or spiritualized it into mere immortality of soul (chap. 15). Corinth was immature, unstable, and unhealthy, not a model church! It was there that glossolalia was most prized.

*Why Corinth?* Why was glossolalia a problem at

Corinth and not, so far as the records go, in other Pauline churches? No conclusive answer has been found. Religious and cultural factors in Ephesus, for example, seem to have been sufficiently like those at Corinth to leave unanswered the question, "Why Corinth and not Ephesus?" There is no certain evidence of unintelligible, ecstatic utterance in pagan life at Corinth as antecedent to the Christian phenomenon.[22]

Possibly the "enthusiasts" within the Corinthian church were under Gnostic influence. Their pride over incest, a man living with his father's wife (I Cor. 5: 1-2), seems to be best understood as reflecting a Gnostic holiness doctrine that one who is in the Spirit or who has higher "knowledge" of God is above sin. Spiritualizing resurrection into a bodiless immortality of soul (chap. 15) may also reflect Gnostic influence. The truth is that though much is known of the fact and nature of tongues at Corinth, there is no certain clue to the causal factors peculiar to Corinth behind the phenomenon.

*Paul's Ecstatic Experience.* Paul himself no doubt contributed to the very phenomenon which he felt compelled to control. He made much of the Spirit, and he referred to "visions and revelations of the Lord" and to one's having been "caught up to the third heaven" where he heard "things that cannot be told, which man may not utter" (II Cor. 12:1-4). Presumably Paul was describing his own experience, remembered over a fourteen-year period. Whatever its nature or whatever its importance to Paul, he limited this to the privacy of his own life, not requiring it as normative for other people and not building his theology upon it. With his charismatic emphasis and possibly occasional ecstatic experience, his balanced judgment of spiritual gifts is apparent in I Cor. 12–14 and Gal. 5:22.

It is significant that although Paul made much of the Holy Spirit, only in I Corinthians does he mention speaking in tongues. Romans gives major attention to the work of the Spirit (5:5; 7:6; 8:2; 6-14, 26-28; 14:17), but it does not mention tongues. The same holds for II Corinthians (3:3, 18; 5:1-5) and Galatians (4:6-7; 5:22-23). In I Corinthians there may even be the recognition that "spirit filled" people, confusing some other spirit with the Holy Spirit, may say, "Jesus be cursed" (12:3).[23]

*Corinth and Pentecost.* It is not defensible to identify the "tongues" at Corinth with what Luke describes at Pentecost. What Luke described was marked by intelligibility. Tongues at Corinth were unintelligible. In Luke's description, "speaking with tongues" at Pentecost was bound up with preaching the gospel, winning people to Christ, close-knit fellowship (*koinonia*), teaching, praying, and sacrificial and joyful living. At Corinth was a sickness almost unto death. The shame of Corinth is not to be cloaked with the glory of Pentecost. Babbling, ancient or modern, is Corinthian and not Pentecostal.

If source criticism leads one to conclude that underneath Luke's narrative an older tradition understood glossolalia at Jerusalem as unintelligible, then he must identify the Corinthian phenomenon with what Luke suppressed and not with what he described.

*Antecedents.* There are traces of ecstatic utterance

41

before the Christian era. The phenomenon was found among some of the early Hebrew prophets, "the professionalized *nebi'im* who, as Yahweh enthusiasts, wandered about the country in bands, working themselves into religious frenzy by means of music and dancing (I Sam. 10:5-13; 19:18-24; II Sam. 6:13-17; I Kings 20:35-37)." [24] Although debated, glossolalia as at Corinth may have corresponded to the ecstatic babblings which caused these prophets to be called *nabi'*. The Dionysian cult may also have known ecstatic states, characterized by frenzy and speech unintelligible except to the initiated and induced by the emotional pressures of ceremonial rites. But demonstration for pagan antecedents to "speaking in tongues" is elusive and uncertain.

Wilder sees glossolalia as emerging among "believers who were so carried out of themselves that they felt impelled to transcend human language and to commune in the language of angels or other mantic articulation," but he sees this tendency as exceptional.[25] Jesus showed no inclination toward glossolalia. He scorned the "babbling" and "much speaking" of pagans (Matt. 6:7). He sometimes chose to be silent (Matt. 27:14; Mark 15: 4-5; Luke 23:9; John 19:9-10), and never was he accused of unintelligible, ecstatic utterance. His "groaning" (KJV) at the grave of Lazarus may best be understood as a normal emotional response, having nothing to do with glossolalia (John 11:33). The "groanings which cannot be uttered" (KJV) with which the Spirit makes intercession for us (Rom. 8:26) have to do with hopes and longings which are too deep for words, and it is not likely that this has any reference to glossolalia.

With Christ came a new age and a new dynamic, and the gospel came as a "speech event" which forged new forms of utterance (e.g., the gospel form as a new literary genre), but Jesus and the apostles spoke through the "secular media of ordinary speech," Aramaic and Greek. The gospel required no "language of Zion," no "Holy Ghost language," no peculiar Christian tongue, no heavenly discourse, but was spoken and written in the language of ordinary people.[26]

*The Fruit of the Spirit.* The Holy Spirit is God's gift of himself to every person who has the openness of faith to receive him. The Holy Spirit is not the exclusive possession of a privileged few. There is no surer evidence that one is stranger to God than the pride which thinks selfishly to possess him. God is nearest the very one who cries out with Peter, "Depart from me, for I am a sinful man, O Lord" (Luke 5:8). He is with one who like the publican cries out, "Be merciful to me a sinner" (Luke 18:13). The Holy Spirit is God himself in his nearness and power within those who trust him. The presence of the Holy Spirit may be seen in terms of the fruit of the Spirit (Gal. 5:22).

When Paul wrote to the Galatians about "the fruit of the Spirit" (5:22), he was not exhaustive in what he listed, but he indicated basic qualities which belong to the cluster of fruit which the Holy Spirit produces in the life in which he dwells: "love, joy, peace, patience, kindness, goodness, faithfulness, gentleness, self-control." Although there is emotional content in such fruit, it is weighted in terms of the moral, ethical, and spiritual.

These are marks of maturity and purpose in persons who are finding true fulfillment. Not the confused and confusing babblings of ecstatic egoism, but just such fruit as Paul commended to the Galatians reflects the coming of the Holy Spirit into the life of a person or community.

# A Brief History of Glossolalia

*E. Glenn Hinson*

Glossolalia has not enjoyed wide currency until recent times. The first sixteen centuries of its history were lean ones indeed. Although we find several references in the early Fathers, they leave us in little doubt about the apparent insignificance of tongues in their day. Some contemporary scholars even doubt whether the Montanists, often cited as the ancient prototype for the Pentecostals, actually practiced glossolalia. Then, if the first five centuries were lean, the next ten were starvation years for the practice in Western Christendom and doubtful ones in Eastern Christendom. The few scattered references to it are dubious in themselves and made even more dubious by the characteristic credulity of the Middle Ages.

A tongues movement began to bud again during the mid-seventeenth century, first among English dissenters and then among the Cévenols in France. For the next two centuries, we can discern new bursts sprouting here and there like prairie grass after a spring shower.

Only in the twentieth century has glossolalia prospered. The last six decades are, in fact, its prosperous years in which numerous Pentecostal denominations have kept the movement alive. Within the last decade also, the practice has received a new shot in the arm from its surprising invasion of non-Pentecostal denominations.

In this chapter,, I shall give as balanced a sketch of the history of tongues as space permits. I believe that we can make a more accurate judgment about its nature by letting the evidence for the movement itself determine our general divisions, and therefore I will avoid the traditional periodizations of church history. Instead, I will make four divisions which, I hope, will give an impression of the impact of the phenomenon on Christian history. Recalling the common twentieth-century designation "The Latter Rain Movement," I decided to use headings which play on the phrase for each of the four periods. Accordingly, I will call the first period, from the first through the fourth centuries, Early Showers; the second, from the fifth through the sixteenth centuries, the Long Drought; the third, from the seventeenth through the nineteenth centuries, Later Showers; and the fourth, from about 1900 on, the Latter Rain.

In a concluding section, I shall make some attempt to evaluate glossolalia in terms of our historical evidence for it.

## I. EARLY SHOWERS

The early Fathers referred infrequently to the gift of tongues, whether ecstatic speech or foreign languages uttered without prior acquaintance or training. We find allusions to it regarding the Montanists, in five well-known authors, and in the spurious ending to the Gospel according to Mark, 16:9-20.

The earliest clear evidence for glossolalia after the New Testament era concerns Montanus, a converted priest of a Phrygian mystery cult, and two of his followers. According to the description of Apollinaris, Bishop of Hierapolis (ca. A.D. 170), Montanus "became beside himself, and being suddenly in a sort of frenzy and ecstasy, he raved, and began to babble and utter strange things, prophesying in a manner contrary to the constant custom of the Church." Later, Apollinaris reported further, he enlisted two women whom he filled with "the false spirit," "so that they talked wildly and unreasonably and strangely," like Montanus himself.[1]

The Montanists, as Bonwetsch[2] has pointed out, do not seem to have stressed glossolalia so much as the ecstatic nature of prophecy. Montanus himself boasted prophetic inspiration. "See, man is as a lyre and I play thereon as a plectron," Epiphanius of Salamis (ca. 374-77) charged him with saying: "Man sleeps and I awaken (him). See, it is the Lord who sets human hearts in ecstasy and who in it gives men heart." [3] Prophetic utterances attributed to Montanus and his followers are usually brief, intelligible statements.

Taken as a whole, the evidence would lead us to conclude that the Montanists did practice glossolalia. Tertullian's statement alone, cited below, suffices to affirm that. However, prophetic inspiration was not, in their minds, the gift of all. Tertullian, for example, nowhere claimed that he possessed it. Rather, he saw it as the special gift of a few like Montanus, Priscilla, Maximilla, and the "sisters" of whom he spoke.

Irenaeus, Bishop of Lyons in Gaul during the last quarter of the second century, referred to tongue speaking three times. In one passage, he cited its occurrence at Pentecost (Acts 2) without comment.[4] In a second passage, he applied it to the ability to speak foreign languages. Alluding to Paul's declaration that "we speak wisdom among them that are perfect" (I Cor. 2:6; KJV), he explained that the word "perfect" means those "who have received the Spirit of God, and who through the Spirit of God do speak in all languages, as he (Paul) used Himself also to speak. In like manner," he continued, "we do also hear many brethren in the Church, who possess prophetic gifts, and who through the Spirit speak all kinds of languages, and bring to light for the general benefit the hidden things of men, and declare the mysteries of God." [5]

In the third passage, Irenaeus told about an abuse of "prophetic gifts" and incidentally may have supplied one reason for the disappearance of tongue speaking a century or so later. A certain Marcus, apparently an early Gnostic, seduced gullible women of means by promising the gift of prophecy. His "sales pitch," according to Irenaeus, went something like this:

I am eager to make thee a partaker of my Charis (spiritual gift), since the Father of all doth continually behold thy angel before His face. Now the place of thy angel is among us: it behooves us to become one. Receive from me and by me [the gift of] Charis. Adorn thyself as a bride who is expecting her bridegroom, that thou mayest be what I am, and I what thou art. Establish the germ of light in thy nuptial chamber. Receive from me a spouse, and become receptive of him, while thou art received by him. Behold Charis has descended upon thee; open thy mouth and prophesy.

When the woman protested, "I have never at any time prophesied, nor do I know how to prophesy," Marcus prompted her further. Feigning certain invocations, he said, "Open thy mouth, speak whatsoever occurs to thee, and thou shalt prophesy." With this encouragement, continued Irenaeus,

She then, vainly puffed up and elated by these words, and greatly excited in soul by the expectation that it is herself who is to prophesy, her heart beating violently [from emotion], reaches the requisite pitch of audacity, and idly as well as impudently utters some nonsense as it happens to occur to her, such as might be expected from one heated by an empty spirit. . . . Henceforth, she reckons herself a prophetess, and expresses her thanks to Marcus for having imparted to her of his own Charis.[6]

The great African theologian Tertullian, himself a Montanist from around 206 until his death sometime after 220, has only one definite and positive reference to glossolalia. In his famous treatise *Against Marcion*, written shortly after his conversion to Montanism, Tertullian cited the evidences of spiritual gifts as a proof of God's oneness and as a refutation of Marcion's doctrine of two gods—the God of Wrath in the Old Testament and the God of Love revealed in Jesus of Nazareth. He concluded this argument with a challenge:

Let Marcion then exhibit, as gifts of his god, some prophets, such as have not spoken by human sense, but with the Spirit of God, such as have both predicted things to come, and have made manifest the secrets of the heart; let him produce a psalm, a vision, a prayer—only let it be by the Spirit, in an ecstasy, that is, in a rapture, whenever an interpretation of tongues has occurred to him; let him show to me also that any woman of boastful tongue in his community has ever prophesied from amongst those specially holy sisters of his. Now all these signs (of spiritual gifts) are forthcoming from my side without any difficulty, and they agree, too, with the rules, and the dispensations, and the instructions of the Creator; therefore without doubt the Christ, and the Spirit, and the apostle, belong severally to my God.[7]

Two statements in Origen would seem to indicate a somewhat hazy acquaintance with glossolalia in his day, the early third century. Once he alluded to foreign languages, once to ecstatic speech. Citing Paul's admission that, "I speak in tongues more than you all," Origen commented, "I suppose that he was made debtor to different nations, because, through the grace of the Holy Spirit, he had received the gift of speaking in the languages of all nations." [8] In his famous apology, Origen had to reply to the pagan philosopher Celsus' charge, evidently aimed at Montanist seers, that some Christian prophets uttered all sorts of nonsense. They made exaggerated claims about themselves, asserted Celsus, saying, "I am God; I am the Son of God; or, I am the Divine Spirit; I have come because the world is perishing, and you, O men, are perishing for your iniquities. But I wish to save you, and you shall see me returning again with heavenly power. Blessed is he who does me homage." After threatening to call down fire from heaven, Celsus continued, they added "strange, fanatical, and quite unintelligible words, of which no rational person can find the meaning: for so dark are they, as to have no meaning at all; but they give occasion to every fool or impostor to apply them to suit his own purposes." [9]

Both Chrysostom and Augustine made it clear that they did not have firsthand experience with the phenomenon. Commenting in a sermon on I Cor. 12:1 ff., Chrysostom remarked, "This whole place is very obscure; but the obscurity is produced by our ignorance of the facts referred to and by their cessation, being such as then used to occur but now no longer take place." [10] In a later sermon on I Cor. 12:27, he underlined strongly Paul's subordination of tongue speaking to other "gifts," noting repeatedly that "he everywhere assigns it the last rank." [11]

Augustine also dismissed the practice as a thing of the past. "These were signs adapted to the time," he observed in his exposition of I John 3:24. "For there behooved to be that betokening of the Holy Spirit in all tongues, to shew that the Gospel of God was to run through all tongues over the whole earth. That thing was done for a betokening, and it passed away." In later times, Augustine noted further, the Spirit manifested himself in other ways, notably in Christian love. "In the laying on of hands now, that persons may receive the Holy Ghost, do we look that they should speak with tongues?" he wanted to know.

Or when we laid the hand on these infants, did each one of you look to see whether they would speak with tongues, and, when he saw that they did not speak with tongues, was any of you so wrong-minded as to say, These have not received the Holy Ghost; for, had they received, they would speak with tongues as was the case in those times?" [12]

Similarly, in his anti-Donatist treatise *On Baptism,* he repeated his statement. The receiving of the Holy Spirit brings the gift of love, something which the Donatists lacked, judging by their disregard of the unity of the church. Thus, concluded Augustine, he was right in asserting that the Holy Spirit is received only in the Catholic Church.

For the Holy Spirit is not only given by the laying on of hands amid the testimony of temporal sensible miracles, as He was given in former days to be the credentials of a rudimentary faith, and for the extension of the first beginnings of the Church. For who expects in these days that those on whom hands are laid that they may receive the Holy Spirit should forthwith begin to speak with tongues. [13]

# A Brief History of Glossolalia

The combined evidence of Chrysostom and Augustine would indicate that tongue speaking had passed off the scene by the late fourth century in both East and West. Chrysostom, at one time a deacon and presbyter in Antioch (381-97) and later Patriarch of Constantinople (397-407), would probably have had direct knowledge if the phenomenon had occurred anywhere in the East. Augustine, who had resided in Rome and Milan several years (383-89) before initiating a long ministry in Hippo (391–430), would have had similar information about its occurrence in the West. Both spoke as if glossolalia had not occurred since very early times.

The Marcan reference to glossolalia, "they will speak in new tongues" (16:17), is difficult to date. Because it appears in the Vulgate, the Marcan addition must have been composed before 380-82, when Jerome prepared the Vulgate edition of the Gospels. It is likely that the passage dates back to the late second or early third century, for it was cited already in the Latin text of Irenaeus' *Against Heresies*.[14] The latter has been dated as early as A.D. 200 and as late as 396. The whole fragment has much similarity to statements about spiritual gifts in Irenaeus and Tertullian, making the earlier date the likely one.

If we can trust such scanty evidence, we have to conclude that glossolalia probably occurred only intermittently and in a restricted manner in the early church. By the last quarter of the fourth century, perhaps before, it had ceased entirely. Since we have evidence of its existence in the early third century, we can safely assume that its demise occurred between *ca.* A.D. 250 and 350.

The unfamiliarity of both Chrysostom and Augustine would make the earlier date seem more likely.

This strange history prompts us to ask two questions: First, why did it occur at all and what was its value? Second, why did it disappear?

The first question probably has to be answered in connection with the beginnings of glossolalia in earliest Christianity. The outburst at Corinth (I Cor. 12–14) undoubtedly was a confirmation of spiritual inspiration against pagan claims to inspiration; the nearest would have been the Delphic oracle. One suspects that a similar thing happened in Montanism. Tongue speaking and other forms of ecstatic speech were confirmation of the validity of the Montanist claims. It is doubtful that the Montanists borrowed the practice from Phrygian mantic prophecy. On the contrary, as Wilhelm Schepelern has demonstrated, they countered the claims of the latter by their own prophetic gifts.[15] Statements of Irenaeus, Tertullian, and Origen would confirm this. Recall, for example, Tertullian's challenge to Marcion. If Marcion would "prove" his doctrine, demands Tertullian, let him "exhibit, as gifts of his god, some prophets, such as have not spoken by human sense, but with the Spirit of God." [16]

While the reasoning behind this type of apologetic may seem strange to us today, it would not have been to the man of the first several centuries A.D. Unless he were an intellectual, he would have had a healthy respect for demonic beings of various descriptions. The Christian saw himself engaged in a vigorous struggle against demonic beings. He responded, as H. Weinel has shown, with his own display of power, not of demons but of the Spirit.[17] Observe, for example, the connection of displays of power, like calling down fire from heaven, with what Celsus called "strange, fanatical, and quite unintelligible words."

Here, however, we begin to see also the reason for the disappearance of glossolalia as an apologetic method. It was difficult indeed to determine whether inspiration of this sort might come from demons or from the Holy Spirit of God! Celsus, who had written his anti-Christian polemic at the very peak of Montanist activity, *ca.* 178, ascribed it to demons. "It is by the names of certain demons, and by the use of incantations," he asserted, "that the Christians appear to be possessed of (miraculous) power." [18]

Distinguishing between spiritual and demonic power was made more difficult by the fact that all and sundry laid claim to spiritual inspiration—charlatans like Marcus, the Montanist seers, Gnostics, and out and out tricksters. Thus, Irenaeus' opinion about Marcus is understandable. "It appears probable enough," he reflected, "that this man possesses a demon as his familiar spirit, by means of whom he seems able to prophesy, and also enables as many as he counts worthy to be partakers of his Charis themselves to prophesy." [19] The Gnostics seem to have made much use of magical or semimagical formulas which were akin to glossolalia. These are particularly noteworthy in the *Pistis Sophia,* part IV. Schepelern cites from the latter a "prayer" of Jesus which contains the following incantation:

Hear me, my Father, You the Father of all Fatherhood, You of endless light: aeaiouo, iao, aoi, psinother, thernops, nopsiter, zagoura, pagoura, nethmomaoth, nepsiomaoth, marachachtha, thobarrabau, tharnachachan, zorokothora, ieou sabaoth.[20]

Strikingly similar formulas appear in the so-called "magical papyri."

In the final analysis, then, glossolalia brought its own downfall. There simply was no way to validate it. The gifts of the Spirit were better, and more safely, attested in positive fruits like "love, joy, peace, patience, kindness, goodness, faithfulness, gentleness, self-control" (Gal. 5:22-23). Over these the church had some control. The more ecstatic forms had to disappear and with them those who depended so heavily on them for their validation—the Montanists and the Gnostics.

## II. THE LONG DROUGHT

From the early fifth century through the entire medieval era, evidences for tongue speaking are scanty at best. In Western Christendom, these are confined mostly to accounts of the ability to speak foreign languages which had not been learned. The surprising thing, in view of the general credulity of the medieval era, is that there are so *few* reports. We have the most complete record in J. J. Görres' *Die christliche Mystik.*

Görres listed among recipients of the "gift of (foreign) tongues" St. Anthony of Padua (1195-1231), Ange Clarenus (in 1300), St. Vincent Ferrier (1350-1419), St. Stephen (Missionary to Georgia), St. Colette (d. 1447), Jeanne of the Cross, St. Francis Xavier (1506-52), St.

Louis Bertrand (1526-81), and others.[21] G. B. Cutten has added also the name of St. Hildegard (1098-1179).

The difficulty of accepting such accounts is pointed up in the story of Francis Xavier. Throughout his letters, Xavier stressed the difficulties he had communicating with different tribes. He tried numerous approaches—translating some of the main church formulas into the language after he had learned enough of the language to do this, getting help from others to patch together some doctrinal statements to be memorized, employing interpreters, mixing various dialects, or even using signs. Xavier's "gift of tongues" was apparently not mentioned until his canonization under Urban VIII (1623-44), almost a century after his death. After this, the legend grew. By 1872, the Jesuit Father Coleridge could sum up Xavier's Japanese ministry by saying, "He spoke freely, flowingly, elegantly, as if he had lived in Japan all his life." [22] The complete inaccuracy of this statement has been demonstrated more recently by a Jesuit scholar, Father George Schurhammer, who attributed the legend to the imagination of two unreliable witnesses in the beatification process.[23]

At the very most, we could claim no more than infrequent individual occurrences of tongues for the medieval era in the West. But what about the East?

Morton Kelsey supposes that the East would be much more receptive than the West due to its mystical, individualistic, otherworldly, introverted piety. "While historical evidence of tongues within the Greek tradition has not been compiled," he concludes, "it is a fair inference that tongue speaking, being no more bizarre

57

than other Eastern monastic practice, has simply continued within the tradition of Greek monasticism without attracting much notice." [24]

My colleague Dr. Dale Moody confirms Kelsey's conjecture. In private conversation, Moody reports, Orthodox monks have narrated direct experiences. They consider these traditional and not uncommon, extending back through the centuries, perhaps even through the Middle Ages. How extensive are they? How far back do they go? It is impossible to say, since no systematic investigation has been done. However, the mystical piety of Easterners could well operate as a sort of dampener for *frequent* extraordinary manifestations like tongues. The *hesychasm* of Mt. Athos, for instance, in which the monk seeks a vision of the divine light through methodical contemplation of the divine, would likely eliminate the need for further phenomenal validation as through tongues.

As we look back over the first sixteen centuries of Christian history, then, we have to reaffirm our conclusion that they were "lean" years for tongue speaking. After the mid-third century, in fact, glossolalia occurred spasmodically, even if it had not ceased entirely. Before that, it was never a major phenomenon. Relatively few claimed it as their "gift." Those who did claim it had to use it with great caution, for they found it difficult to distinguish from demonic inspiration.

But the story is about to change. In the late seventeenth century a revival took place. For two centuries we see an outburst first in one place, then in another. Let us now turn to this phase of the story.

## III. LATER SHOWERS

In the seventeenth to the nineteenth centuries, there were two noteworthy outbursts of tongue speaking, one in France, the other in England. Besides these, the phenomenon also seems to have accompanied the revival movements of the same era.

### The Cévenols

The first widespread incidence of glossolalia occurred in southern France. It followed in the wake of the revocation of the Edict of Nantes by Louis XIV in 1685 and a fresh outburst of persecution of the French Huguenots.

The revocation forbade both private and public worship apart from the Roman Catholic churches, enjoined ministers to embrace the Roman faith or leave the country, prohibited Protestant schools, ordered the baptism of children of Protestant parents by Catholic clergy and their education in parochial schools, and threatened men with conscription for the galleys and women with imprisonment and confiscation of property. The pent-up contempt of Catholics for the Protestant "heresy," long restrained by the Edict of Nantes, burst like a swollen dam. Cleric, magistrate, soldier, and private citizen all joined in one grand mêlée to reestablish Catholicism as the national faith.

Parts of the country which had a heavy Protestant populace did not easily succumb to threats and force, however. The Huguenots resisted, first quietly and then violently. Not unexpectedly, this generated further suppression and counterviolence.

Among those who resisted most stoutly were the peasants of Languedoc province who dwelt in the Cévennes Mountains. Inheritors of the free spirit of the Albigenses who had once resided in the same area, they steadfastly maintained their right to worship according to the dictates of conscience. Under the most distressing conditions of poverty and terror a sort of religious hysteria seized some of them.

The Cévenol peasants first reported hearing the singing of psalms in the air. Later, after their antagonists had refused to believe their reports, "the poor shepherds" brought forward something more tangible. They claimed prophetic inspiration.

Among the first to make this boast, in 1688, was a young girl named Isabeau Vincent, a wool-carder's daughter. Though familiar only with the native *patois,* when seized by ecstatic trance, the young girl was reported to have prophesied for hours in perfectly cultivated French.

Subsequently, as the fervor of persecution heightened, reports of spiritual inspiration increased, touching all ages and both sexes. Various physical phenomena accompanied it—convulsions, foaming at the mouth, sobbing, and glossolalia. One of the most surprising things was its incidence among small children, even infants.[25]

The increasing severity of the persecution led in the end to a fanatical revolt among the Cévenols. Some of the more able and aggressive leaders gathered an army known as the Camisards in 1702. Knowing the mountainous terrain well, they inflicted heavy losses on the royal armies dispatched to wipe them out. So successful were they, in fact, that the French authorities finally had to grant considerable concessions in 1704. In the process, though, the Cévenols had suffered irreplaceable losses. By 1710 their resistance came to an end.

## The Irvingites

The second major outburst of tongues occurred in England during the nineteenth century. This movement crystallized around a dashing, eloquent Scottish Presbyterian pastor in London named Edward Irving. By nature, Irving (1792–1834) was a mystic and charismatic. Several years before the emergence of glossolalia in Irving's Newman Street Church, London, his distinguished poet friend Thomas Carlyle expressed genuine puzzlement about his preaching and his personal habits. "I do not think he will go altogether mad," he mused, "yet what else he will do I cannot so well conjecture. Cant and enthusiasm are strangely commingled in him." [26]

Strangely enough, it was not Irving who first spoke in tongues. He, in fact, never received the "gift" which he so earnestly sought. The initial outburst took place in Fernicarry, Scotland, where a young farm girl, Mary Campbell, was snatched miraculously from death's door and claimed prophetic inspiration in 1830. Others of her acquaintances likewise experienced tongues and gifts of healing.

To Irving this was an answer to prayer. He hastened to Scotland to observe firsthand what he had heard about. What he found there, he sought to have duplicated in his London congregation. According to his wish, a tongues movement broke out in London, recorded first on April 30, 1831. Irving wisely sought at first to keep its manifestation private. It was not long, however, until he found it difficult to restrain those gifted with it. News of it spread like wildfire. In November, 1831, he vowed never again to forbid its public exercise.

Edward Irving himself soon encountered bad times. Recently cleared of a heresy charged to his doctrine of the person of Christ, he was summoned a second time before his presbytery, this time for allowing women and men not properly ordained to speak in church. The charge was obviously aimed at the outburst of glossolalia which he not only permitted but even encouraged. Accordingly, he was deposed in May, 1832, and less than a year later defrocked and excommunicated by the Church of Scotland.

A broken man, Irving returned to his church and humbly accepted the office of deacon. A circle of his colleagues headed by Henry Drummond, an English banker, had already taken charge. Drummond and other notables in the circle founded the Catholic Apostolic Church, which mixed Catholic with millenarian and pentecostal tendencies. Tongue speaking has occurred less frequently in later times but is still reported in the movement.[27]

# A Brief History of Glossolalia

## The Revival Movements

During these same centuries also, glossolalia was occurring now and then in the revival movements of England and colonial America. The seventeenth through the nineteenth centuries were, in fact, particularly fruitful periods for religious enthusiasm in its varied forms. It is difficult to estimate the *extent* to which glossolalia occurred, however, for these popular movements often went unreported or were reported only by detractors.

The Ranters, who flourished during the Commonwealth era (1648-60) along with a large number of other sects, seem to have been fond of glossolalia and other types of extravagant speech, as their name would imply. Unfortunately, we know little about them. They apparently had few checks on their spiritual enthusiasm. Samuel Fisher, a contemporary, charged, "Some Ranters are not ashamed to say that they are Christ and God, and there is no other God than they, and what's in them, and such like blasphemies." [28] The charge is reminiscent of that made against the Montanists.

Similarly, the early Quakers probably witnessed tongue speaking as one of many expressions of the Spirit's power in their lives. Fox and his followers often reported visions, groaning, quaking or trembling, weeping, outbursts of prophecy, foaming at the mouth, faintings, and the like as a result of their meetings. Quakers got their name, of course, from the jerking spasms which they experienced when under strong religious emotion. In his *Journal*, Fox reports several times his defense of these evidences of the Spirit. However, the Friends them-

63

selves later minimized glossolalia. They placed their primary emphasis on intelligible prophecy. Yet, in spite of that, their doctrine of the inner light opened the way for all sorts of peculiar manifestations of the Spirit.

Early Methodism also had some experience with extraordinary spiritual phenomena, especially in Northern England and Wales. Their occurrences were significant enough, in fact, that John Wesley had to take up the pen against critics. When Dr. Conyers Middleton charged in his attack on miracles that the gift of tongues had not occurred since apostolic times, Wesley refreshed his memory by citing its occurrence among the Cévenols.

Reports of unusual spiritual happenings increased as the revivals gained momentum. They became more and more frequent as the Wesleys resorted to a lay ministry to bolster their efforts. Both in his *Journal* and in *A Short History of the People Called Methodists,* Wesley quoted an account of a revival meeting in Huntingdonshire in May, 1759, by the Rev. Mr. J. Beverridge, in which both adults and children fell under the power of the Spirit. They shrieked, swooned, fell to the floor as if dead, babbled senselessly, cried out in praise of God, and so on. If Wesley had momentary qualms about their authenticity, he quickly put them out of mind. In response to his own sense of danger "to regard extraordinary circumstances too much," Wesley said, "Perhaps the danger *is,* to regard them too little." [29]

It was perhaps this positive attitude toward spiritual gifts on the part of Wesley and his followers which helped most to pave the way for modern Pentecostalism, for the modern-day movement has its roots in the revivals of the eighteenth and nineteenth centuries in America. The Great Awakening and subsequent revivals produced some unusual by-products, of which tongue speaking was undoubtedly one. Spirited preaching, singing, physical movement, and the demand for a tangible display of the receiving of the Spirit worked together to create astounding physical demonstrations. Barking, violent jerking, shrieking and shouting, wild dancing, fainting, and the like were common. One of the notable evangelists of the frontier revivals, John McGee, related a not untypical incident which occurred in the summer of 1799:

William (John's brother) felt such a power come over him that he quit his seat and sat down on the floor of the pulpit, I suppose not knowing what he did. A power which caused me to tremble was upon me. There was a solemn weeping all over the house. At length I rose up and exhorted them to let the Lord God Omnipotent reign in their hearts, and their souls should live. Many broke the silence. The woman in the east end of the house shouted tremendously. I left the pulpit and went through the audience shouting and exhorting with all possible ecstasy and energy, and the floor was soon covered with the slain.[30]

The evangelical revivals, both in England and America, had a broad impact. The charismatic displays which accompanied them left their mark on numerous sects. The Shakers are a prime example.

As heirs both of Quaker and Wesleyan tenets, it is natural to expect that the Shakers would have charismatic leanings. The founder of this movement, Mother Ann Lee, was a visionary. Migrating from England to America about 1774, she and her followers settled first in New York, then moved elsewhere. They played a considerable role in the late eighteenth-century revivals in Kentucky. Their chiliastic and spiritualistic emphases lent themselves quite handily to a sort of Pentecostalism. According to their *Summary View of the Millennial Church,* published in 1848, they regarded tongues, dancing, and various ecstatic states as the highest expressions of worship.

The Mormons, likewise heirs of revivalism, also cultivated the charismatic gifts, including tongue speaking. *The Book of Mormon* leaves little doubt about its approval by the prophetic and visionary founder of the movement, Joseph Smith. The gift of tongues and their interpretation are mentioned several times, each time with strong approbation. Deniers of these gifts, said the prophet, know not the gospel (Mormon 9:7). Small wonder, then, that the Mormon constitution affirmed, "We believe in the gift of tongues, prophecy, revelation, visions, healing, interpretation of tongues, etc." [31] Hence, though in recent years Mormon leaders have tended to minimize glossolalia, it has never been forbidden.

Even Roman Catholics have had a bout with tongues. The Jansenists of France had a notable outburst in 1731. The negative reaction of the church only intensified it; but it was squelched quickly through the aid of the French state authorities.[32]

## IV. THE LATTER RAIN

In the twentieth century the Pentecostal showers of an earlier day have given way to a steady rain, first in the founding of the Pentecostal churches, more recently in its development in non-Pentecostal denominations. Before looking at these in historical perspective, however, let us examine its earlier roots.

### Antecedents

In essence, the Pentecostal movement developed as a partial reaction to the increase of secularism and the subsequent waning of revivalism following the Civil War. Its immediate ancestor was the holiness or perfectionist movement within Methodism occasioned by a controversy over John Wesley's doctrine of sanctification.

Wesley had had much to say about sanctification; in fact, it was one of the keystones in his theology. He seems to have taught the "progressive sanctification" of believers, that is, their gradual growth toward perfection. However, he conceded also to some of his followers that the Christian can attain perfection in love even while he lives, citing I John 4:17. At the same time, he insisted, contrary to those who rejected out of hand the doctrine of "entire sanctification," that "we should expect to be saved from all sin before the article of death." [33] This uncertainty in Wesley's thought opened the way for later debate.

Some Methodists stressed the doctrine of "entire sanctification," that is, the immediate and complete perfec-

67

tion of love in the believer, and organized revivals designed to lead to it. By 1867 this movement had gained such a large following as to alarm Methodist leaders. Between 1880 and 1900 Methodists split into holiness and antiholiness factions. The holiness groups gradually separated from the Methodist Church.

## THE PENTECOSTAL CHURCHES

In the wake of this turmoil the Pentecostal movement also began. It was related to, but not the same as, the holiness movement. Both, of course, were concerned about sanctification. But whereas the latter stressed complete perfection or entire sanctification, the Pentecostals stressed charismatic gifts.

Several Pentecostal revivals, accompanied by tongue speaking, sprang up almost simultaneously in the United States just after the turn of the twentieth century. Their fundamentals, called the "Foursquare Gospel," were entire sanctification, baptism of the Holy Ghost as evidenced in tongue speaking, faith healing, and the premillennial coming of Christ. In the minds of early adherents the incidence of these in their day fulfilled the prophecy of Joel 2:23 ff. concerning the "latter rain."

The latter rain fell first in Topeka, Kansas, in 1901. The movement took shape around the founder and leader of Bethel Bible College, Charles F. Parham. On New Year's Day, 1901, the "baptism of the Spirit" fell first upon Miss Agnes N. Ozman, a student in the college, who claimed to speak several languages. Parham's baptism came on January 3 along with that of other students. Filled with new zeal, Bethel students set out to evangelize Kansas and to share their newly found power. By 1903 the movement reached into Missouri and Texas. Parham himself opened a Bible school in Houston, Texas, in 1905.

In 1906, the latter rain hit Los Angeles. As it did, the movement began to take on international proportions. Preceding and probably helping to prepare the way for it there were some direct offshoots of the holiness movement, notably the Church of the Nazarene, founded in Los Angeles in 1895. W. J. Seymour, a Negro holiness preacher who had attended the Bible college in Houston, took over the reins of the movement, even though he had not been the first to experience the baptism of the Spirit and probably had not experienced it before he came to Los Angeles.[34] His baptism occurred on April 12, 1906. A week later, Seymour and his followers, who had first gathered in a home on North Bonnie Brae Street, moved into a rented building at 312 Azusa Street, which had formerly served as a Methodist church. Here the Press "got wind" of the then unusual revival and gave free advertisement. Pentecostalism grew wings.

From Los Angeles the Pentecostal movement spread to Chicago, New York, and elsewhere in the U.S.A. and Canada. Before the end of 1906, there were Pentecostals also in India, Norway, and Sweden.

Pentecostalism has obviously had its finest hour in the country of its birth. In his superb study of *The Pentecostal Movement,* Nils Bloch-Hoell noted that in 1955 thirty-six Pentecostal bodies reported a combined membership of slightly under one and a half million.

Besides these, there were twenty-three other Pentecostal organizations which listed no statistics.[35]

Pentecostals have also done surprisingly well in the Scandinavian countries. The movement was brought first to Norway by a Norwegian Methodist pastor, T. B. Barratt, who came to the United States in 1905 to raise funds for his Oslo City Mission. After an ecstatic experience in October, 1906, and an experience of tongues on December 26, he became its European apostle. From Oslo the tongues movement spread throughout Norway and finally to other parts of Europe.

## TONGUE SPEAKING AMONG NON-PENTECOSTALS

Glossolalia among non-Pentecostals is so new that its story can hardly be told. As indicated in Chapter I, it was not until 1960 that the movement became public knowledge. Yet today we encounter reports of its occurrence more than a decade ago, which fear of censure and harrassment kept suppressed until now.

Since this 1960 episode, many others have reported experiences with glossolalia. The movement has touched several denominations and all walks of life. Although reports have come from many denominations, three—Episcopalians, Presbyterians, and Baptists—have been most affected. Contrary to the expectation of some, tongue speaking has not been confined to the lower economic, social, and cultural strata with whom we usually associate Pentecostalism. Physicians, lawyers, teachers, business executives, and other professionals have humbly joined the swelling chorus of laborers, factory workers, farmers, and the like who speak and sing God's praises in an unknown tongue. Pentecostals no doubt look with obvious satisfaction upon the masses who once scoffed but now bear witness along with them to the "baptism of the Spirit."

## V. SOME REFLECTIONS ON THE HISTORY OF GLOSSOLALIA

As we gaze in retrospect at the history of glossolalia, we are inclined naturally to ask: Is it possible to discern any sort of pattern or to interpret the movement in terms of its history? Our answer to the question is likely to be less positive than we should like. The greatest consistency lies, I think, in causes. There is much less consistency in constituency and characteristics. Let us examine briefly each of these.

With reference to *causes,* the circumstances surrounding an outbreak of glossolalia in various centuries have been similar, though not identical. In the patristic period and among the Cévenols, it burst forth in a time of persecution and severe repression. Otherwise, it arose in a period of declining religious interest. This applies particularly to the seventeenth century and after in England and America, when deism and skepticism had their heyday.

These two situations perhaps share enough common elements to suggest one major reason for the manifestation of tongues. Both have to do with the restraining or repressing of religion—one by active and the other by passive resistance. Glossolalia and other perceptible evidences of the Spirit could thus be seen as an effort to convince unbelievers by a display of power, if not of word! Careful study of statements of those who claimed to speak in tongues will support this statement. It was this kind of confirmation, for example, which Tertullian the Montanist demanded from Marcion to back up his claims as an interpreter of Christianity. The Cévenols, the Ranters, the early Quakers, the revivalists, the modern Pentecostals—all followed suit in calling upon tongues to bear witness to the truth in their spiritual experience.

With reference to *constituency,* Pentecostalism has been less consistent. It has undoubtedly drawn its greatest following from the masses, the lower economic and social strata with limited education. Yet one can cite among its strongest proponents some from the higher economic, social, and cultural levels. Tertullian was a well-educated Roman lawyer before his conversion to Christianity. The Jansenists belonged to the intellectual elite of eighteenth-century France. Edward Irving and his circle moved about easily in British high society. Early Methodism attracted people from all ranks. The present movement among non-Pentecostals covers a wide economic, social, and cultural range.

In view of the indefiniteness here, it may be more fruitful to examine personality traits. Dr. Wayne Oates can undoubtedly make a more accurate judgment here on the basis of modern case studies, but perhaps one observation based on historical evidence would not be out of place. Those who have experienced or nurtured glossolalia cannot be fitted into a single stereotype. They represent diverse, often opposite, personalities. Tertullian, for example, judging from his own writings and others' descriptions of him, was a man of considerable abilities and training, a rigid puritan who demanded visible evidence of Christian commitment. For him, glossolalia supplied authority. In sharp contrast, Charles F. Parham, wellspring of the modern Pentecostal churches, was a man of limited abilities and culture whose personal morality was suspect. For him, glossolalia supplied assurance. With inconsistent data, it is perhaps best to keep in mind John Wesley's self-admonition that we count tongues and other ecstatic phenomena neither too little nor too much.

With reference to the *nature* of the Pentecostal movement, it has been rather common to regard it as typical ecstatic emotionalism. The tag fits in some cases; in others it does not. The Cévenols, severely persecuted as they were, were stricken with intense emotion. They became almost lunatic in their opposition to Catholic and state authorities. The Quakers, revivalists, Shakers, and modern Pentecostals have defended emotion as a healthy feature of religion. Yet, emotionalism has not accompanied all occurrences of tongues. The Montanists, if Tertullian is an example of their constituency, were not intensely emotional. The Irvingites had a mild admixture of emotion which seldom went beyond the control of leaders, although Irving once confessed that he had difficulty restraining its devotees in public worship. Morton Kelsey has argued on the basis of contemporary evidence that while "tongues *can* occur in a highly charged atmosphere, . . . *the unleashing of emotionalism is simply not a necessary part of speaking in tongues."* [36]

Factionalism has often been charged to Pentecostals. The history of the movement would undoubtedly lend some weight to the charge. Yet factionalism has not resulted from one side alone. New sects have resulted as frequently from the unwillingness of the majority to accept the minority as from undue pride or inherent factional tendencies among the spiritualists. So many factors can and have contributed to divisions within Christendom that it would not be fair to these movements to single them out for censure. Where leaders have been willing to tolerate considerable diversity within their ranks, the rift developed more slowly. A case in point is the long history of diversity within Methodism; it was not until the line hardened that the final split occurred.

If we view glossolalia more positively, we are immediately confronted with a problem. If it is indeed to be seen as an evidence of the Holy Spirit's work, why did it have such an inconsistent and intermittent history? Again, if it were as significant as Pentecostals maintain, would it not have occurred regularly and without letup throughout the many centuries of Christian history? Could it ever have been so suppressed by action of the church that clear evidences could not always have been seen?

Thus we reach a rather uncertain conclusion. If tongues and other phenomenal spiritual gifts have not hurt the church, neither have they helped particularly in the accomplishment of the church's mission. Tongues and the like have perhaps startled the unbelieving, but they have not always convinced them. Where they have become too highly regarded by Christians, they have caused offense and their users have been charged with demonry. The best advice to those who "speak in other tongues" would be: Use it for your own edification, but take care lest you make of the gospel a greater offense than need be! The best advice for those who do not have this gift would be: Seek other ways to express the power of the Spirit in the church, but do not suppress and harrass those who claim these gifts, lest you quench the Spirit in your zeal for orderliness and uniformity!

# A Socio-Psychological Study of Glossolalia

*Wayne E. Oates*

The recent breakthrough of speaking in tongues has both spontaneity and organization within the Christian fellowship. This breakthrough both happens of itself and is caused by plan. Both as a happening and as an organized plan, the phenomenon can be studied empirically from a socio-psychological point of view. It can be brought into relationship with what we know about the psychological development of language in human life and the character of human language as a social expression of the individual's need for other people. The apostle Paul, in referring to the phenomenon, says that "he who speaks in a tongue edifies himself," and goes on to say, "but he who prophesies edifies the church" (I Cor. 14:4). The former is a highly personal kind of edification and the latter highly social. Indirectly the apostle Paul speaks of the phenomenon of speaking in tongues as a childlike way of communication. Nevertheless, he does say directly that speaking in tongues can be a form of private prayer to God. (I Cor. 13:11; 14:2.) One therefore might well assume a hypothesis: speaking in tongues is "cradle speech" of the newborn Christian. It may be likened to the language of children. The persons who speaks in tongues cannot be "written off" as a fanatic, a sick person, or a fool. We do not know how to pray as we ought. Therefore, these tongue speakings may be the "sighs too deep for words." On the other hand, they may become extremely meaningful to us personally whether they mean anything else to anyone else at all notwithstanding.

Yet when we immediately "write off" speaking in tongues with such pejorative impatience and say that it is immature, childish, and, therefore, of no worth, we are being just as harsh and judgmental as if we reject the language of children because it is a babbling and not understandable. Newborn infants have no language but a cry. At the same time, however, the careful and disciplined psychologist and psychotherapist would not be so hasty or judgmental. The language of a child is important. Certain psychologists and psychotherapists have devoted much of their lives to the objective study of children's language. Others have made careful note of the role of language in the development of personality. The purpose of this paper, therefore, is to correlate the studies of these psychologists with what we know about speaking in tongues as a childlike form of language. At the outset of the paper a hypothesis will be set forth as to the reasons why present-day religious milieu has lent itself to both the spontaneous and organized expressions of speaking in tongues. The second part of the paper will be devoted to a study of the development of speech in children as compared with speaking in tongues. The final part will deal with some pastoral approaches to the problems of speaking in tongues based on the conclusions of the first two parts of the paper.

## WHY SPEAKING IN TONGUES NOW?

Speaking publicly about religious matters today has certain elements of taboo surrounding it. We are supposed to be a scientific people. As David C. McClelland has said: "To admit a religious point of view, to some personal commitment, is to violate the most fundamental rule governing the behavior of a scientist—namely to be objective." McClelland goes on to say that

the taboo on religion holds for more than those who should remain professionally objective. Very few intellectuals in my circle of any kind take Christianity seriously except as an historical or social phenomenon. . . . A psychological colleague of mine has told me that the same condition exists among undergraduates. He has found in his intensive study of a number of them that they talk readily enough about their sex lives, but unwillingly and with great hesitation about their religious convictions. He has concluded that it is not sex which is a delicate subject in our generation but religion.[1]

We must notice that this taboo particularly holds among sophisticated, upper middle-class, professional persons. Shyness and inarticulateness focus more upon religion than sex. Victorian repression excluded sex from our conversation. Mid-century secular society represses and selectively ignores religion in reference to God, except as a joke or as profanity. The easy, spontaneous discussion of religion, particularly in its intimate personal aspects, no longer exists. It takes "brashness," "directness," and even "compulsiveness" to speak openly of God in many circles today. Even the courage to speak of God directly and personally as nurtured by the neo-evangelicals such as Billy Graham and by theological institutions has a sort of forced necessity about it. The milieu in which we live has become overwhelmingly inarticulate about God especially in the home, the place where language is learned initially. As Paul M. van Buren has put it, "Our inherited language of the supernatural has indeed died 'the death of a thousand qualifications.' "[2]

On a broader cultural base than the home, the effort to maintain separation of church and state in the field of public education has also contributed to the conspiracy of silence about God and personal faith. Here is, next to the home, the most important fountain of learning to speak,—the public school. Yet the verbalization of religious feeling, the discussion of religious ideas, and the performance of religious acts are by law forbidden. This is not to say that the burden of religious education *should* be shifted from the home and the church to the public school. Rather, it is merely to say that one of the "side effects" of separation of church and state is to render growing young persons inarticulate about their faith at the time of their most intensive study of the language of their native tongue.

But the churches themselves have also contributed to the conspiracy of silence about personal faith from several angles of vision. In the first place, the churches have from the beginning been social gathering places as well as congregations for the spoken and communal worship of God. They have been the company of the respectable and "the better off" people of the land. As a result, the informal conversation and dialogue from member to member has tended to be focused upon social and civic affairs rather than upon specifically personal religious experiences. The adaptation of religious concepts to personal meaning, the reflective criticism of religious truths and feelings, the formulation and answering of religious questions is not the substance of the "after meeting" conversations of communicants. These matters are "too personal" and "too private" to discuss. They are touchy and approached only with queasy feelings of uneasiness. The conspiracy of silence about personal religious experience prevails, then, even at the level of one-to-one conversation in the church. At the very personal level, even the most faithful church attendant would have great trouble in uttering a public prayer, in expressing his faith to his fellow church members, and in putting into words some of his deepest religious feelings.

One scene in the movie *The Slender Thread* tragically portrays the ways in which social superficiality of church gatherings obscures the depth of people's concerns and leaves their life and death struggles for survival and for the reality of God untouched. A woman, her husband, and her son attend church after many years of not having done so. The week before, the woman's husband had discovered inadvertently that the boy who he had always thought was his son was actually that of another man by his wife. She had withheld this from him for over twelve years. He rejected her and she went into a profound mood of dispair. For some reason, however, they all went to church the next Sunday. The service was over. Everyone left the sanctuary except the man and his wife. The man asked: "Why did we come here?" The woman replied: "I don't know." At that moment a member of the church reentered and said: "'You'd better come on and hurry. We're having cake and coffee. Won't you join us for some fellowship?"

Thus ended a conversation that did not know where to begin at the outset. The main issues of sin and salvation, life and death, despair and hope were obscured by the superficial chatter of a coffee and cake routine. The desperation of human beings speaking out of the depth to be heard in the depth—deep calling unto deep—was "sicklied o'er" by the coffee and cake socialization.

One would expect things to be different in theological schools. But the theological students, and their teachers as well, more often than not come from the kind of homes, schools, and churches about which we have been speaking here. The student brings a religious shyness with him also. He brings a furtive diffuseness as to why he wants to be a minister and is not clear about his religious purpose. He has deep feelings, but he has never learned to articulate them or to focus them in such a way that they can be understood either by himself or by others. Particularly is this true of the student and the professor who come from the middle classes of our society. In theological schools, the data and controversies of Christian ideology in institutions are studied with fiercely objective acumen. Historical precision and critical clarity are developed to a high level of skill. However, the curriculum and the economic pressures under which students and faculty work leave little room or opportunity for the small group exploration of the personal religious life of both students and faculty. The articulation of intense spiritual concerns falls back upon efforts at counseling with the student individually or upon the barren ground of total inattention. The conspiracy of silence about personal religion prevails even in the theological school as it does in the home and the lower echelon schools—the appearance of being less religious than one really is. The blasé attempt to be "secular" bears psychological evidence of a "protesting-too-much" kind of reaction against the deeper strivings that brought the persons to the theological school in the first place, either as a student or as a professor.

Seen from a psychoanalytic perspective, this "unspeakableness" concerning God, Christ, the Holy Spirit, religious decision, and personal commitment has all the earmarks of repression. Repression functions through other mechanisms of denial, isolation, undoing and reaction. The attempt to appear irreligious smacks of various forms of repression. The inarticulateness is more than a conspiracy of silence in the presence of others. It may be a denial of the presence of God at the level of the unconscious. The task of the spiritual director, then, is to uncover these repressed concerns of which many other problems which have hitherto been considered basic are indeed only symptomatic. In the absence of this kind of uncovering and surfacing of deeper religious passions, these needs may erupt into turbulent upheavals and expressions of pent-up feelings, such as we find in speaking in tongues. Attendant upon this eruption may be a variety of other types of "ununderstandable" kinds of behavior. In other words, the person may do many things, not just one thing, that do not make sense. The temper of our times has called forth the emergence of the phenomenon of speaking in tongues. Some persons' feelings finally break forth and "they have no language but a cry." Yet the cry itself, like the first scream of the newborn babe, is a sign of life and should be taken seriously, however childlike. The formulations of psychologists and psychotherapists concerning the seriousness and importance of the movement of a child's language from private unintelligibility to social communicability provide helpful clues for appreciating and dealing realistically with the "unknown" tongues of the glossolalics.

# LANGUAGE AND THE THOUGHT OF THE CHILD

This socio-cultural backdrop helps to explain why speaking in tongues today has broken out not in the wake of persecution but, rather, amid widespread social acceptance of popular religion. Yet this popular religion is superficial. It is social to the point of being impersonal. Again, speaking in tongues today has broken out not in the wake of depression and economic privation, as in the strong emergence of Pentecostalism during the Depression years. Instead it has broken out in the wake of affluence. The symbols of affluence—money, cars, television, radio, hi-fi, boats, vacation, and more and more elaborate homes—nevertheless do not substitute for the simplicities and depth of personal communication between family members, neighbors, and fellow churchmen. In fact, many of these symbols, particularly television, have had a way of short-circuiting and blacking out communication. Family members substitute watching one another's behavior, much as they watch television, for talking and listening to one another in the home. Church members substitute watching what others do and have for talking with others about the central issues of being a Christian. This "watching" behavior as a substitute for verbal communication has become the main motif of an affluent social order in its pattern of communication. But eyes are not enough for adequate communication. Words must be used and ears in order to complete the process. If at all possible, the nostrils and the fingertips must be involved in a total expression

84

of the individual's communicative capacities—seeing, hearing, smelling, touching, and tasting. However, in our affluent society we are restricted to one set of senses—the eyes—either to watch others or to read about them, not to communicate verbally with them. Furthermore, the phenomenon of speaking in tongues has broken out not among the unwashed and unbaptized but among the sophisticated, the early baptized, and the "chronically" religious—ministers, ministers' sons, theological students, and affluent professional and business people. It has an atmosphere and air of prestige and affluence which it has never known before.

As speaking in tongues actually expresses itself, however, it is a childlike, unguided, and unpatterned kind of speech. It is untranslatable and is meaningful to the person experiencing it in much the same way that the first utterances of a small child are meaningful to him. A study of speaking in tongues comparative with the development of language in the thought of the child, therefore, is appropriate here.

Jean Piaget studied for many years the development of language and thought as a primarily qualitative experience in the character development of a child. Piaget was born in Switzerland in 1896. He taught philosophy, psychology, and the history of scientific thought, first in Switzerland and later at the Institute for Advanced Studies at Princeton University.

Piaget and a colleague together examined minutely the language of two children of six years of age at the *Maison des Petits de L'Institut Rousseau*. They classified the speech of these children into two categories—*ego-*

*centric speech and socialized speech.* When a child speaks ego-centrically he utters phrases and does not bother to know to whom he is speaking and does not care whether or not he is being listened to. As Piaget says:

He talks either for himself or for the pleasure of associating anyone who happens to be there with the activity of the moment. This talk is ego-centric, partly because the child speaks only about himself, but chiefly because he does not attempt to place himself at the point of view of his hearer.

The child does not desire to influence his hearer, to tell him anything, to be understood by him, but speaks for the sheer joy of speaking for its own sake. Sardonically enough, Piaget likens this to "drawing-room conversation where everyone talks about himself and no one listens." [3]

Piaget divides or classifies ego-centric speech into three categories. The first one is *repetition* (*echolalia*). Here the child uses only a conglomeration of words and syllables, repeats them for the pleasure of talking and with no need to make sense to anyone else. Much that we find in the stream of speech of the glossolalic is repetitive speech of this kind. It is devoid of any social character. However, it is internally satisfying to the glossolalic, much as baby prattle is internally satisfying to the small baby.

The second category is *monologue*. Here the child talks to himself. He thinks aloud. His address is to no one. A recent psychologist, B. F. Skinner, calls this "the speaker as his own listener." [4] It is a remarkably rich kind of language, he points out, because the language of the speaker and that of the listener are exactly the same. No time is lost in transmission, translation, and semantic dillydally. Obviously this "inner community" can "drift toward disturbing idiosyncrasies," but the "outsider" cannot ignore with impunity what is going on. Such verbal behavior has definite practical effects upon the speaker in his monologue. Skinner says that "self-mands" are uttered here which determine the actions of the person. Autistic behavior springs from autistic speech. Much that has enriched our culture in the form of soliloquies consists of this kind of speech. At its heart it is asocial. Another person reading it projects *his* meaning upon the words. He can only aver that this *was,* in deed and in fact, the meaning of the writer. An excellent example of this kind of writing most recently appeared in Dag Hammarskjöld's *Markings.* It was Hammarskjöld who said that "the more faithfully you listen to the voice within you, the better you will hear what is sounding outside. And only he who listens can speak." [5]

As a third category, Piaget describes ego-centric speech as being *dual or collective monologue:* He recognizes that this is a contradiction of terms but uses the contradiction to underline the paradoxes of those conversations between children "where an outsider is always associated with the action or thought of the moment, *but is expected neither to attend nor to understand."* Here the child simply never takes into account either the view of the other person or the presence of the other person. Presence of the other person serves simply as a stimulus to the speech, and no response is expected.

Speaking in tongues could not be more accurately

described. Outsiders are indeed and in fact associated with the speaking. They may serve as the stimulus of the speech. But it is a part of the covenant that they neither understand nor attend. Piaget calls this a "secret" and a "mystery." [6] He goes further in his discussion of the functions of child language and says that in contradistinction to ego-centric speech there is *socialized speech*. Socialized speech consists of initial, adapted information in which the child really exchanges his thoughts with others. The child is concerned with interesting others and influencing their actions. He is concerned with developing a common aim with them. He tries to adopt the point of view of his hearer. Moreover, socialized speech contains *criticism,* a word taken not in the ethical sense but in the sense that the child speaks so as to create an argument or develop emulation and copying. From this point of vantage, speaking in tongues may be characterized as socialized speech, because whole groups of people participate and are at the same time interested in interchanging ideas about speaking in tongues. They develop common aims and are much concerned about being understood. Their speaking can certainly be characterized as criticism, since they give rise to arguments or quarrels, and create emulation and imitation. The whole earlier Pentecostal movement was a movement of this type of socialized use of speaking in tongues.

Again, Piaget says that socialized speech is demonstrated in the commands, requests, and threats that we express one to another. It is demonstrated in the questions we ask and answers we give. Therefore, socialized speech becomes dialogical in these three additional respects. Again we see that the commands, requests, and threats of a small group who have become enthusiastic about speaking in tongues do provoke questions in those around them and require answers of the people who do speak in tongues. Publications in the contemporary tongue-speaking movement attempt to answer some of the questions raised and offer admonitions for those who have not "come along with the 'movement.'" Therefore, on the basis of Piaget's findings concerning the nature of children, we can say that by analogy speaking in tongues is not solely an autistic, ego-centric expression of childlike language but also an attempt at socialization. This attempt takes on the form of institutionalization when a group is established and clarified by publication or explanation. The modest flow of literature coming from the present-day "speakers in tongues" indicates the residue of the educational results of previous religious training. For example, John L. Sherrill in his book *They Speak With Other Tongues* emphasizes at the outset the development of resonance between two people and tries to answer not only his own questions about the experience of speaking in tongues but also the questions of others. He insists on looking behind the language and mannerisms of the glossolalics to see their joy and their life. He is concerned that such an expenditure of spiritual energy not become ego-centric. On the other hand, he is equally concerned that "pattern is essential in all true growth." The energy of the glossolalic without plan and structure would be unedifying and nonproductive. He puts it this way: "If growing things had only energy without plan, we would never see such end products as an oak tree or a human being or a full spiritual life." [7]

Another contemporary psychologist has contributed materially to the understanding of language in the development of personality. Harry Stack Sullivan in his book entitled *An Interpersonal Theory of Psychiatry* underscores the interactional dimensions of human personality by focusing on a person's development in relation to other people. Communication is the essence of being human. Consequently, the development of speech is one of the most important gauges to the growth of the person. Sullivan divides the earliest phases of the human being into three eras or modes of experience. These three modes begin in infancy and perdure throughout life. The first mode of experience is the prototaxic one, before the appearance of any attempt at audible speech. Here the child literally has no language but weeping, no language but a cry. Crying and breathing are his means of communicating with his environment in his absolute helplessness. The second phase or mode of experience is the parataxic one, in which the child begins to utter, however unintelligibly to others, forms of speech that are pleasant and meaningful to him. These forms of speech have definite meaning to the individual child and are idiosyncratic to him alone. They correlate with Piaget's description of ego-centric speech. The struggle and the conflict between mother and child at this stage are those of the mother learning to identify what these private sounds really mean. Distortions of the inner meanings of this era perdure throughout life and are called "parataxic distortions." When they appear in adult interactions, conflict attends them. Hostility, anxiety, withdrawal, etc. emerge in personal interaction. Conventional psychoanalytic thinkers speak of regression to infantilisms; Sullivan would speak of parataxic distortions that need to be clarified at the adult level. Sullivan's third level or mode of experience is the syntaxic mode. Here the child learns to make his own language correspond meaningfully with that of people around him. He "consensually validates" his meaning with that of other people. Understanding develops. Relationship grows. Community is built. The glossolalic is pushed and pressed by the apostle Paul to make himself understood by others. This moves him to a higher level of maturity as he edifies the church and not just himself. Consensual validation is necessary for any genuinely steadfast community life.[8]

In an age in which we are so profoundly inarticulate about religion, the earliest emergences of religious experience tend to stir up the oldest parataxic distortions, to use Sullivan's concept. Confusion, failures of communication, and stuporous inarticulateness accompany deep religious experiences in many instances. What "comes out" to the rest of the world "does not make sense." Seen from this perspective, speaking with tongues has all the characteristics of having tapped the wells of parataxic distortion which go all the way back to the era of one's most elemental attempts to communicate with other people.

Two other psychoanalysts help us in understanding these parataxic distortions even further. Erik Erikson says that at this phase of infantile development one is

establishing "basic trust" of other people. The conduit
of basic trust is verbal communication. The insulator
of basic trust is the failure or refusal to communicate.
The development of speech is a security operation for
the sake of learning to trust other people. If religious
experience is profound, if it does plumb the depth and
not just scratch the surface of human experience, it is
little wonder that persons whose deepest religious strivings have been repressed through sophistication, intellec-
tualization, institutionalization, and the superficial over-
lay of social behavior will break forth into highly dis-
torted and seemingly meaningless babblings of the sort
described by glossolalics. The suspicion with which they
are viewed and with which they view the world puts to
test the original issue of their development: can they
genuinely trust other people and be trusted by them? [9]

Beyond and behind the inability of a person to trust
other people is the larger issue of his own self-sufficiency.
Can he get along without others very well? The person
who decides that he does not need other people because
they cannot be genuinely trusted develops a grandiose
conception of himself as a substitute for community.
This grandiosity—the Bible calls it pride—is a dividing
line among the glossolalics themselves. Some of them
are vaunted with pride. Others have deep need of their
fellowmen and are openly expressive of this need. Some
groups of glossolalics create in-groups that do not allow
others to enter and exalt themselves overmuch as they
compare themselves with others. The out-group is to be
suspected. This line divides the relatively healthy glossolalic from the person who is psycho-pathologically

involved in his experience. One cannot make the generalization that all glossolalics are mentally ill. Nor can one draw the equally false assumption that all of them have a unique degree of health. The findings of Sullivan and Erikson concerning the development of personality give us a guideline in understanding something of the psychopathology of glossolalic behavior.

## GLOSSOLALIA AND MENTAL ILLNESS

Clinical psychiatric contact with persons who demonstrate both symptoms of mental illness and expressions of speaking in tongues teaches us much about this phenomenon. James N. Lapsley and John H. Simpson have surveyed this problem and describe speaking in tongues as "a form of dissociation within the personality, in which a set of voluntary muscles respond to control centers other than those associated with consciousness." [10] There are many mental states in which this response of voluntary muscles occurs. In such states a buildup of tension takes place in which the muscular structure associated with the voluntary nervous system becomes tighter and tighter. The normal way of relaxing these muscles is through sleep. In sleep the voluntary muscles are relaxed through control centers other than those associated with consciousness. Another normal way of relaxing these consciously controlled muscular structures is through the experience of sexual orgasm. Here the voluntary muscles are built to a state of excitement and tension and in orgasm are relaxed dramatically. A more diffuse and less focalized form of relaxation of voluntary

93

muscles through control centers other than those associated with consciousness is in mass or mob activity. In the mass activity of a highly exciting football game great crowds of people are built to a state of excitement and tension and relief through either the joy of "their side having won" or through the despair of "their side having lost." John Sherrill points out how our culture has disseminated some of its religious concern in these directions. It is perfectly appropriate and normal to become ecstatic on some occasions, but it is gruesome to see a similar buildup of tension in the mob action of race riots in this country. Here conscious control is turned over to a mass activity, and one "throws his mind out of gear and lets himself go where he is pushed." In the psychiatric treatment of mentally disturbed persons, the release of this tension can be brought about in several different ways. The methods are highly controlled, and the predictability of their outcome is a common criterion of their worth. The first method in the treatment of psychiatric patients is hypnosis, which was originally used by Freud and by Bleuler. Very early Freud discarded the use of hypnosis and turned to a milder and longer term method of release of these tensions through free association in the exploration of the nonverbal and more repressed aspects of one's being. A second method of release was used in World War II with soldiers suffering from gross stress reactions in combat. Through the use in small quantities of sodium amytal and sodium pentothal, a controlled condition similar to that of hypnosis could be produced. The patient could go back and talk through and talk out the experience of trauma which had disabled him, and be released from the bondage of his more conscious experience.

Two of the most common techniques of release of tension of voluntary muscles through control centers other than those associated with consciousness are electro-convulsive and insulin-convulsive therapy used today by psychiatrists. This is a highly controlled kind of release procedure. The objective of it is to produce an element of release at the conscious level by "getting at" some of the less conscious controls of the personality.

More recently the use of the psychotropic drugs, commonly known as tranquilizers, has become another method of medically releasing the tension of the voluntary muscles by affecting the involuntary or autonomic nervous system through the use of chemotherapy.

In the experience of speaking in tongues there seems to be a conglomeration of several of these nonmedical approaches to releasing the tension of the voluntary muscular situation of a person. There is certainly a buildup of tension, there is hypnotic impact of a mass or a group, and there is the ecstatic release of tension.

This release, as in the case of the indications of medical types of therapy, often comes in the midst of a syndrome of psychiatric symptoms. One of the most common reactions of mentally sick persons with the speaking-in-tongues "solution" is a schizophrenic reaction of a paranoid type. Here you find a person, as has already been indicated, suffering with deep feelings of suspicion and distrust of the world about him and, at the same time, entertaining elaborate and grandiose conceptions of himself which are severed from any appropriate emotional association. Usually the mentally sick glossolalic is also highly isolated and may have only inadvertently or accidentally become involved in an older, more ritualized and group-centered kind of Pentecostal or neo-Pentecostal glossolalic group. Underlying these grandiose and suspicious feelings are quite often specific guilt feelings that prompt the individual to exhibitionistic acts. From my clinical observation, exhibititionism tends to be a hallmark of the glossolalic who is suffering from a psychotic reaction. The rituals of exhibitionism tend to be isolated forms of a "private religion" in which the person "confesses" his weakness to the community and receives punishment in the same act. From a pastoral point of view, it is important that the act be seen as a confession of guilt and that it be handled nonpunitively and therapeutically rather than as a "crime against society." Whereas the pastor or other type of counselor may not always have these options at hand nor have the cooperation of the patient, this is nevertheless a fond hope to be sought for and a clinical intention to be realized.

In an unpublished paper, Andrew D. Lester has aptly said that along with these exhibitionistic tendencies "another symptom of regressive behavior among glossolalics is childish megalomania. Feelings of omnipotence and ego-centricity are often exhibited." The group to which such persons belong may provide a religious context for exercising leadership which other contexts do not provide. In his firsthand visitation of glossolalic groups, Lester observed that the people with whom he talked had weak egos, confused identities, high levels of anxiety, and unstable personality. They had chaotic religious backgrounds and a remarkable degree of emotional deprivation. Emotional deprivation does not follow socio-economic lines. It appears in the homes of the most affluent where communication is nonexistent and where clear expressions of open trust are absent.

The terrible isolation and loneliness of successful people in the middle-class churches has broken out in other forms and manners in this generation. The hyperdependence upon alcohol, the high incidence of psychosomatic disorders, the absence of a clear-cut family structure, and the conventionalization of the church life all provide a fertile soil for the sudden chaotic breakthrough represented in glossolalia.

## SOME PASTORAL IMPLICATIONS OF GLOSSOLALICS

Usually pastors do not deal with a problem such as that of glossolalics until an individual or a small group emerges within their own particular congregation. An important procedure, therefore, would be for the pastor to anticipate the problems and to discuss with his congregation in small groups the meaning of speaking in tongues. The articles by Professors Stagg and Hinson provide biblical and historical background, while this article gives the psychological background for discussions in such groups. They should be two-way discussions and deal with the basic facts concerning biblical teaching, historical manifestation, psychological issues at stake, and pastoral problems of the care of souls. These facts should be discussed sympathetically, objectively, and without easy, careless, and nonchalant disregard for the persons of the glossolalics as individuals for whom Christ has died. Furthermore, the church should take a close look at its own superficiality. Are the deep problems of life and death, such as those presented by the couple in the movie *The Slender Thread,* being glossed over and ignored in the "coffee and cake routine" of the average church? Is the church providing adequate small-group opportunities for persons to explore their own religious pilgrimage and to develop a more intimate and profound ability to discuss their religious experiences? Are individuals being enabled to put into words how they feel about God? Are their doubts, fears, and anxieties about their own religious experiences simply smiled over, smiled through, or smiled around? If this is true, then the church itself is leaving the unresolved tensions of people untouched and unmollified. No normal and creative expressions of an understandable order are being provided, and sooner or later a "breakthrough" will take place. Whether the breakthrough is in a speaking-in-tongues movement, an open conflict with the established leadership, a conflict over a social issue such as racism or John Birchism or not, the breakthrough will inevitably come. Therefore, an alert pastor will be sensitive to these possibilities and provide outlets and openings for the expression of the deepest feelings of his people.

But in spite of all that a pastor can do, and beyond all that a wise leadership of a Christian fellowship can commandeer, experiences of glossolalia will emerge nevertheless. When this does in fact happen, it is important that the pastor and the leadership of the church not feed the needs for persecution that such a group may have. Furthermore, it is important that some place and opportunity for expression may be given. It is important that every effort be made to understand the deepest needs of the persons involved, and every discipline be exercised to require that they make themselves understandable. This means that pastor and deacons, elders, stewards, or vestrymen, as the case may be, take an approach of sympathetic listening, create openings of communion and fellowship through nonjudgmental efforts, and be on their own guard lest they underestimate the vitality and creativity of such persons.

Finally, the congregation should have the wisdom and guidance of the pastor from the pulpit about the work and place of the Holy Spirit. A solid biblical exegesis of the work and ministry of the Holy Spirit would bring this and all other types of "un-understandable behavior" within the life of the church into a clearer focus. My concluding suggestion is that a thoroughgoing reaffirmation of the total doctrine of the Holy Spirit and its function in the life of the church is the best antidote for the problems, needs, and creativity presented by glossolalics within the life of the church.

# NOTES

## Why a Book on Glossolalia Today?

1. Quoted by Harold Bredesen, "Discovery at Yale," *Trinity* (Christmastide, 1962-63).
2. James W. L. Hills, "The New Pentecostalism: Its Pioneers and Promoters," *Eternity* (July, 1963), p. 18.
3. *The New Pentecost Charismatic Revival Seminar Report,* FGBMFI, 1963, pp. 16-18.
4. *Ibid.,* p. 9.
5. See James A. Pike, "Pastoral Letter Regarding 'Speaking in Tongues,'" *Pastoral Psychology* (May, 1964), pp. 56-61.
6. *Tongue Speaking* (Garden City, N. Y.: Doubleday & Co., 1964), p. 231.

## Glossolalia in the New Testament

1. Cf. Johannes Behm, "Tongues, Other Tongues," *Theological Dictionary of the New Testament,* ed. by Gerhard Kittel; tr.

by G. W. Bromily (Grand Rapids, Michigan: Wm. B. Eerdmans Publishing Co., 1964), I, 719-27.

2. Walter Bauer, *A Greek-English Lexicon of the New Testament and Other Early Christian Literature,* tr. and ed. by W. F. Arndt and F. W. Gingrich (Chicago: The University of Chicago Press, 1957), p. 161.

3. Behm, "Tongues, Other Tongues," *loc. cit.,* p. 721.

4. Bauer, *A Greek-English Lexicon of the New Testament and Other Early Christian Literature,* p. 161.

5. Cf. B. F. Wescott and F. J. A. Hort, *The New Testament in the Original Greek* (New York: Harper & Bros., 1882), II, 28-51; A. T. Robertson, *Studies in Mark's Gospel* (New York: The Macmillan Company, 1919), p. 216; Vincent Taylor, *The Gospel according to St. Mark* (New York: The Macmillan Company, 1957), pp. 610, 614-15; B. M. Metzger, *The Text of the New Testament* (New York: Oxford University Press, 1964), pp. 226-29; *et al.*

6. See below, pp. 29-31.

7. *See* Stewart D. Currie, "Speaking in Tongues: Early Evidence outside the New Testament Bearing on 'Glossais Lalein,'" *Interpretation,* XIX (1965), 274-94, for four possible meanings: (1) speaking a human language one has not learned, (2) speaking a non-human language, (3) uttering a dark saying, more enigmatic than prophecy or revelation and requiring interpretation, and (4) uttering cadences of vocalization which do not constitute discourse (p. 294). He finds first- and second-century evidence for the third expression and concludes that if the fourth expression occurred it was easily mistaken for charlatanry, sorcery, or some other magical practice, and that its exercise was unpublicized or unrecorded. He sees "interpretation" as either (1) translation of what was uttered into a common language of the hearers, (2) exegesis or explanation of words that were intelligible but obscure, or (3) "interpretation" in the sense of what an art critic sees in painting or music, i.e., an explanation of the mood (praise, lament, thanksgiving, exultation) of the utterance (p. 275).

8. Kirsopp Lake, "The Gift of the Spirit in the Day of Pentecost," *The Beginnings of Christianity,* ed. F. J. Foakes-Jackson and Kirsopp Lake (London: The Macmillan Company, 1933), V, 112, says that Luke clearly identifies glossolalia with prophecy in contrast to Paul who distinguishes between them; but

Lake holds that Luke was mistaken about glossolalia, making it intelligible instead of unintelligible. But this follows only if the phenomena at Jerusalem and Corinth were the same, and this has only been theorized from alleged echoes of an alleged underlying source to Luke's story.

9. Behm, "Tongues, Other Tongues," *loc. cit.*

10. A. Q. Morton and G. H. C. MacGregor, *The Structure of Luke and Acts* (New York: Harper & Row, 1965), pp. 36, 44.

11. In 1798, B. L. Königsmann proposed that the author of Luke-Acts was to be distinguished from the author of the "we" passages in Acts (cf. Jacques Dupont, *The Sources of Acts,* tr. by Kathleen Pond [London: Darton, Longman and Todd, 1964], p. 52). In 1891, F. Spitta in *Die Apostelgeschichte, ihre Quellen und deren geschichtlicher Wert,* introduced the theory of two parallel sources in Acts (*ibid.,* p. 33). He proposed that the original narrative mentioned only ecstatic glossolalia (2:1a, 4, 12-13), and the second narrative (2:1b-3, 5-11) contained reference only to the miracle of speaking with intelligible tongues (polyglossia). Thus Spitta is largely responsible for the now widely held position that the original story understood the gift of the Holy Spirit on the day of Pentecost to have been accompanied by unintelligible, ecstatic utterance and that Luke's secondary source was responsible for the alteration of this, so as to refer to intelligible speech.

Harnack built upon and modified the theory of Spitta without directly referring to him (Adolph Harnack, *The Acts of the Apostles,* tr. by J. R. Wilkinson [New York: G. P. Putnam's Sons, 1909], chap. 5 *et passim*). Working with the criterion of setting (scenes and persons) instead of linguistic analysis, he distinguished between two sources in chaps. 1–5. He found 3:1–5:16 to belong to what he termed "Recension A" and to be the earlier and more intelligible history of the giving of the Holy Spirit (*ibid.,* p. 188). He found chaps. 2-3 and 5:17-42 "Recension B" to be secondary filled with doublets, and almost worthless (*ibid.,* pp. 179, 188, 194). He did hold that "Recension B" was "correct in recording that the outpouring of the Holy Spirit was manifested in the 'speaking with tongues,'" this being exaggerated by Luke or by "Recension B" itself (*ibid.,* pp. 194 ff.) Harnack's distaste for miracles apparently played a part in his judgment of what was "correct" and what was not.

12. R. R. Williams, *The Acts of the Apostles,* "The Torch Bible Commentaries" (London: SCM Press, 1953) , p. 39.
13. Ernst Haenchen, *Die Apostelgeschichte* (13th ed., Göttingen: Vandenhoeck & Ruprecht, 1961) , p. 136.
14. "The Gift of the Spirit in the Day of Pentecost," pp. 113-14.
15. *Die Apostelgeschichte,* p. 138.
16. *Ibid.,* p. 137. Haenchen holds that Luke did not find one old and unified tradition about Christ's giving of the Spirit, citing John 20:22 as evidence of a tradition that Christ "breathed" the Holy Spirit upon his disciples. Something of this idea is seen behind Luke's presentation.
17. *Ibid.,* p. 138.
18. *Ibid.*
19. *Ibid.* pp. 138-39.
20. Cf. Frank Stagg, *The Book of Acts, The Early Struggle for an Unhindered Gospel* (Nashville: Broadman Press, 1955) , pp. 54-56, 120, 197.
21. Sidney Cave, *The Gospel of St. Paul* (New York: Harper & Brothers, 1929) , p. 210.
22. Cf. Strabo, *Geography,* VII, 378-82, and Pausanias, *Description of Greece,* II, 27.
23. Cf. Frank W. Beare, "Speaking with Tongues: A Critical Survey of the New Testament Evidence," *Journal of Biblical Literature,* LXXXIII, Part III, 229-46.
24. E. Andrews, "Gift of Tongues," *The Interpreter's Dictionary of the Bible,* ed. G. A. Buttrick (Nashville: Abingdon Press, 1962) , IV, 671-2.
25. Amos N. Wilder, *The Language of the Gospel* (New York: Harper & Row, 1964) , p. 27.
26. *Ibid.,* pp. 26-47.

## A Brief History of Glossolalia

1. Quoted by Eusebius, *Church History,* Vol. 16; *Nicene and Post-Nicene Fathers,* second series, I, 231 (hereafter referred to as *NPNF*) .
2. G. N. Bonwetsch, *Die Geschichte des Montanismus* (Erlangen: A. Deichert, 1881) , pp. 57-58.
3. Epiphanius, *Panarion,* 84. 4.
4. *Against Heresies,* III. 12. 1.
5. *Against Heresies,* V. 6. 1; *Ante-Nicene Fathers;* I, 531 (hereafter referred to as *ANF*) .

6. *Against Heresies*, I. 13. 3; *ANF*, I, 334.

7. *Against Marcion*, V. 8; *ANF*, III, 446-47.

8. Cited by George B. Cutten, *Speaking with Tongues* (New Haven: Yale University Press, 1927), p. 36.

9. *Against Celsus*, VII. 9; *ANF*, IV, 614.

10. Homily XXIX; *NPNF* [1], XII, 168.

11. Homily XXXII; *ibid.*, pp. 186 ff.

12. Homily VI on The First Epistle of John; *NPNF* [1], VII, 497-98.

13. *On Baptism, Against the Donatists*, III. xviii. 16-21; *NPNF* [1], IV, 443.

14. *Against Heresies*, II. 20. 3; III. 10. 5.

15. Wilhelm Schepelern, *Der Montanismus und die Phrygischen Kulte* (Tübingen: J. C. B. Mohr, 1929).

16. *Against Marcion*, V. 8.

17. Heinrich Weinel, *Die Wirkungen des Geistes und der Geister* (Leipzig: J. C. B. Mohr, 1899).

18. Origen, *Against Celsus*, I. 6.

19. *Against Heresies*, I. 13. 3.

20. *Der Montanismus und die Phrygischen Kulte*, p. 157.

21. Quoted at length in Cutten, *Speaking with Tongues*, pp. 37-40.

22. Cited in Cutten, *Speaking with Tongues*, p. 45.

23. *Butler's Lives of the Saints*, ed., rev., and supplemented by Herbert Thruston, S. J., and Donald Attwater (New York: P. J. Kenedy & Sons, 1956), IV, 481.

24. Morton T. Kelsey, *Tongue Speaking* (Garden City, N. Y.: Doubleday & Co., 1964), p. 43.

25. See Henry N. Baird, *The Huguenots and The Revocation of the Edict of Nantes* (London: Kegan Paul, Trench, Trübner & Co., 1895), pp. 182 ff.

26. Letter to John Carlyle, June 10, 1828; quoted by Cutten, *Speaking with Tongues*, p. 89.

27. See Andrew Landale Drummond, *Edward Irving and His Circle* (London: James Clarke & Co., n.d.), p. 234.

28. Quoted by A. H. Newman, "Antinomianism and Antinomian Controversies," (Vol. I of *The New Schaff-Herzog Encyclopedia*), p. 198.

29. *A Short History of the People Called Methodists*, 79; *The Works of the Reverend John Wesley*, John Emory, ed. (New York: Lane & Scott, 1850), VII, 375.

30. Cited by E. T. Clark, *The Small Sects in America* (Nashville: Abingdon Press, 1949), p. 91.

31. Joseph Smith, "Articles of Faith," in *History of the Church,* IV, 541; cited by Thomas F. O'Dea, *The Mormons* (The University of Chicago Press, 1957) , p. 137.
32. *See* Eddison Mosiman, *Das Zungenreden geschichtlich und psychologisch untersucht* (Leipzig: J. B. Hirschfeld, 1911) , pp. 57-58.
33. The Fourth Annual Conference, June 17, 1747; *John Wesley,* Albert Outler, ed. (New York: Oxford University Press, 1964) , p. 168.
34. *See* Nils Bloch-Hoell, *The Pentecostal Movement* (Norway: Universitetsforlaget, 1964) , p. 35.
35. Bloch-Hoell, *The Pentecostal Movement,* p. 56.
36. Kelsey, *Tongue Speaking,* p. 145.

## A Socio-Psychological Study of Glossolalia

1. David C. McClelland, "Religious Overtones in Psychoanalysis," *The Ministry and Mental Health,* Hans Hofmann, ed. (New York: Association Press, 1960) , p. 49.
2. Paul M. van Buren, *The Secular Meaning of the Gospel* (Paperback edition; New York: The Macmillan Company, 1966) , p. 4.
3. Jean Piaget, *The Language and Thought of the Child* (New York: Meridian Books, 1955) , p. 32.
4. B. F. Skinner, *Verbal Behavior* (New York: Appleton-Century-Crofts, 1957) , pp. 438-67.
5. Dag Hammarskjöld, *Markings* (New York: Alfred A. Knopf, 1964) , p. 13.
6. *The Language and Thought of the Child,* pp. 32-33.
7. John L. Sherrill, *They Speak with Other Tongues* (New York: McGraw-Hill Book Company, 1964) , p. 157.
8. *See* Harry Stack Sullivan, *The Interpersonal Theory of Psychiatry* (New York: W. W. Norton & Company, 1953) , pp. 28-30.
9. *See* Erik Erikson, *Childhood and Society* (2nd ed.; New York: W. W. Norton & Company, 1963) , pp. 247-74.
10. James N. Lapsley and John H. Simpson, "Speaking in Tongues," *The Princeton Seminary Bulletin,* LVIII (February, 1965) , p. 6.

# BIBLIOGRAPHY

Bergsma, Stuart. *Speaking with Tongues: Some Physiological and Psychological Implications of Modern Glossolalia.* Grand Rapids, Michigan: Baker Book House, 1965.

Bess, Donovan. " 'Speaking in Tongues': The High Church Heresy," *The Nation,* CXCVII (September 28, 1963), 173-77.

Butterfield, D. W. "Go Ye Out to Meet Him," *Voice,* XIII (December, 1965), 13-15.

Cutten, George Barton. *Speaking with Tongues: Historically and Psychologically Considered.* New Haven, Connecticut: Yale University Press, 1927.

Dalton, Robert Chandler. *Tongues Like as of Fire.* Springfield, Missouri: The Gospel Publishing House, 1945.

Drummond, Andrew Landale. *Edward Irving and His Circle.* London: James Clarke & Company, n.d.

Erikson, Erik. *Childhood and Society*. Second edition. New York: W. W. Norton & Company, 1963.

Farrell, Frank. "Outburst of Tongues: The New Penetration," *Christianity Today*, VII (September 13, 1963), 1163-67.

Frodsham, Stanley. *With Signs Following: The Story of the Pentecostal Revival in the Twentieth Century*. Springfield, Missouri: The Gospel Publishing House, 1941.

Goldsmith, Harry. "The Psychological Usefulness of Glossolalia to the Believer," *View*, II (No. 2, 1965), 7-8.

"Government Grant for Study of 'Speaking in Tongues,' " *Pastoral Psychology*, XV (September, 1964), 53-56.

James, William. *The Varieties of Religious Experience*. New York: Collier Books, 1961.

Kelsey, Morton T. *Tongue Speaking: An Experiment in Spiritual Experience*. Garden City, New York: Doubleday & Company, 1964.

Kendrick, Klaude. *The Promise Fulfilled: A History of the Modern Pentecostal Movement*. Springfield, Missouri: The Gospel Publishing House, 1961.

Lapsley, James N. and Simpson, John H. "Speaking in Tongues," *The Princeton Seminary Bulletin*, LVIII (February, 1965), 1-18.

Lester, Andrew D. "Glossolalia: A Psychological Evaluation." Unpublished seminar paper, Southern Baptist Theological Seminary, Louisville, Kentucky, 1965.

Lhermitte, Jacques Jean. *True and False Possession*. New York: Hawthorn Books, 1963. Trans. by P. J. Hepburne-Scott.

Mackie, Alexander. *The Gift of Tongues: A Study in Pathological Aspects of Christianity*. New York: George H. Doran Company, 1921.

Maglione, Paul B. "I Had Religion," *Voice*, XIII (September, 1965), 19-22.

# BIBLIOGRAPHY

Martin, Sam G. "Time Is Flying," *Voice*, XIII (December, 1965), 6-8.

McClelland, David, C. "Religious Overtones in Psychoanalysis," *The Ministry and Mental Health*, Hans Hofmann, ed. New York: Association Press, 1960, pp. 49-68.

Mezer, Robert R. *Dynamic Psychiatry in Simple Terms*. New York: Springer Publishing Company, 1960.

Murphy, Gardner. *Personality: A Biosocial Approach to Origins and Structure*. New York: Harper & Brothers, 1947.

Oates, Wayne E. "Ecstaticism." Unpublished paper, Duke University, 1943.

Oesterreich, T. K. *Possession: Demoniacal and Other*. New York: Richard R. Smith, 1930.

Oman, John B. "On 'Speaking in Tongues': A Psychological Analysis," *Pastoral Psychology*, XIV (December, 1963), 48-51.

Piaget, Jean. *The Language and Thought of the Child*. New York: Meridian Books, 1955.

Pike, James A. "Pastoral Letter Regarding 'Speaking in Tongues,'" *Pastoral Psychology*, XV (May, 1964), 56-61.

Pratt, James B. *Religious Consciousness: A Psychological Study*. New York: The Macmillan Company, 1921.

"Preliminary Report." Unpublished study by the Division of Pastoral Services of the Episcopal Diocese of California, Study Commission on Glossolalia, 1963. Copies can be obtained from the Diocesan Headquarters at 1055 Taylor Street, San Francisco, California.

Sherrill, John L. *They Speak with Other Tongues*. New York: McGraw-Hill Book Company, 1964.

Skinner, B. F. *Verbal Behavior*. New York: Appleton-Century-Crofts, 1957.

Starbuck, Edwin D. *The Psychology of Religion*. New York: Charles Scribner's Sons, 1914.

Stolee, H. J. *Pentecostalism; the Problem of the Modern Tongues Movement.* Minneapolis, Minnesota: Augsburg Publishing House, 1936.

Sullivan, Harry Stack. *The Interpersonal Theory of Psychiatry.* New York: W. W. Norton & Company, 1953.

Van Buren, Paul M. *The Secular Meaning of the Gospel.* Paperback edition. New York: The Macmillan Company, 1966.

Wilkerson, David. *The Cross and the Switchblade.* New York: (Geis) Random, 1963.